Advance Praise of *The Critical Decade*

"I greatly appreciated the inspiring talks that professor Work delivered during the United Nations Public Service Forums."

—Adriana Alberti,
PhD, Chief, Programme Management and
Capacity Development, Division for Public Institutions
and Digital Government, UN Department
of Economic and Social Affairs (UNDESA)

"Robertson Work's official positions, 16 years at the United Nations Development Programme followed by years at New York University, provided stature for conference keynote addresses. He graciously accommodated many requests but offered something far beyond his titles. He spoke with the urgency and power of a prophet along with the empathy and compassion of a fellow journeyman as he explored our responsibility for the challenges of climate change. He deeply touched his audiences when I personally heard him deliver his call to action. I experienced the same in reading his other talks. Now, new audiences far and wide, will also find their imaginations and conscience stirred. Robertson provided a crucial perspective, and bestowed a treasured gift, when he spoke to ICA veterans gathered during 2010 to consider the future of the organization in international work. His impassioned words focused our attention and instilled renewed confidence at a moment when both were at low ebb. His words continue to speak to those on a journey of service as they face shifting challenges."

—Terry Bergdall,
PhD, CEO ICA-USA, 2009-2015; faculty member,
ABCD Institute, DePaul University, Chicago

"Robertson Work's call to engagement in this critical decade has inspired all who heard him in the halls of power at the United Nations or in 2011 and 2019 at the Building Creative Communities conferences in Colquitt, Georgia, USA. The leaders of rural communities and students from Florida State University were challenged to acknowledge and accept his summons to strategic engagement for the future of the planet. While the spoken word is important as in his speeches, Rob's written words in this book will be treasured by all who read them."

—Joy Jinks,
Co-coordinator, Building Creative
Communities Conference, Colquitt, Georgia

"I strongly recommend this book particularly for development workers, policymakers, and students. Prof. Robertson shares his insights and years of professional experience through talks in several forums. I remember hearing him speak in Kathmandu about creating a viable planet, our chance for breakthrough thinking, doing and being, for innovation, creativity, boldness, and risk-taking at the 8th Global

Conference on Human Development 2012. This book would be an excellent medium to gain an in-depth understanding of compassionate leadership, innovation in self-governance, and development."

—Ishu Subba,
Executive Director, ICA Nepal

"I am so pleased that Robertson Work has included 'The Four Faces of War and Peace: Mindsets, Behaviors, Cultures, Systems,' which he presented at the Oklahoma City University Symposium on Creative Peace Building in 2014. As the primary keynote speaker, Robertson provided the red thread that helped bring the various elements of the conference together as a coherent whole. His combination of expertise and passion in relation to peacemaking in various contexts is a truly remarkable gift that he brings to our world in a time when systemic change for people and the planet is so urgently needed."

—Rev. Dr. Mark Y. A. Davies,
Wimberly Professor of Social and Ecological Ethic,
and Director of the World House Institute,
Oklahoma City University

"In 2019, Rob Work's passionate call to action gave further impetus for ICA/EI archives work to become the basis of a Social Research Center (SRC) where the methods and wisdom used in the years of global experimentation in organizational and community development could be a resource for other movements, helping them to develop strategies to deal with blocks facing all humanity as they work toward a new vision for the future."

—Lynda Cock,
ICA Social Research Center, Chicago

"Each year our multicultural school and community celebrate the UN's International Day of Peace with World Fair Field events. One of the most memorable featured Robertson Work's 2018 keynote address, an all encompassing vision of not only the multiple challenges confronting our global family, but also a roadmap for how progress could be achieved toward all of the UN's SDGs. Interwoven with this global perspective were references to the extraordinary pioneering work of our community in spiritual and sustainability practices. I share with Robertson the hope that these initiatives and more can be replicated to scale, so that we can indeed, 'shock the world with sustainable development,' on every level."

—Dr. Richard Beall,
Co-Head of Maharishi School, Fairfield, Iowa, USA

"From his vantage point of a life dedicated to development, from villages, to the UN, to a university faculty, Rob brings deep insight into our world's situation. He documents in these lectures the big picture of the multiple crises we are experiencing, then offers opportunities for the future in the midst of the crises. Multiple examples and stories of what is possible inspire hope and practical action. Rarely do we find such a powerful articulation of the reality of our situation combined with inspiration to positive action."

—Jo Nelson,
Certified ToP™ Facilitator, ICA Associates, Toronto, Canada

"Can we, as the human race, evolve together as individuals and as communities? Science would tell us that our bodies and our minds are equipped for this task. These 12 talks address this question of the "how to" from different perspectives of lived experience. Based on experience, both local and global, the book invites the human race to participate in this process of evolution. It is a critical decade and the pandemic allows us to see the stark reality of the need. Our global human consciousness is shifting to allow for the birth of a compassionate global civilization. This book is a call to action."

—Mary Kurian D'Souza,
Pune, India

The Critical Decade

Also by Robertson Work

Book author
Earthling Love: Living Poems 1965 - 2020
Serving People & Planet: In Mystery, Love, and Gratitude
A Compassionate Civilization: The Urgency of Sustainable Development and Mindful Activism – Reflections and Recommendations

Chapter author
Changing Lives, Changing Societies
Decentralization and Power-Shift
Engaging Civil Society
Life Lessons for Loving the Way You Live (Chicken Soup for the Soul)
New Regional Development Paradigms: Vol. 3
Reinventing Government for the 21st Century

General editor and contributor
Participatory Local Governance
Pro-Poor Urban Governance: Lessons from LIFE 1992-2005

Contributor
Cities, People and Poverty: UNDP Urban Strategy
Re-conceptualizing Governance
The Urban Environment

The Critical Decade

2020 - 2029

Calls for Ecological-Compassionate Leadership

Robertson Work

Compassionate Civilization Press

ISBN: 978-0-578-78003-0

Library of Congress Control Number: 2020920569

Compassionate Civilization Press
Swannanoa, North Carolina
28778 USA

Dedication

This book is dedicated to five of my master teachers

Joseph Wesley Mathews
Jean Houston, PhD
Ken Wilber
G. Shabbir Cheema, PhD
Larry Ward, PhD

Contents

Preface

What prepared and impelled me in 2010 – 2019 to give twelve talks on the critical decade and the strategic actions and innovative leadership required?

Reading Pierre Teilhard de Chardin in the 1960s was an early influence. He said it this way: "The task before us now, if we would not perish, is to shake off our ancient prejudices, and to build the Earth." Then, there was my grassroots human development work around the world with the nonprofit Institute of Cultural Affairs (ICA) in the 1970s and 80s. One ICA ritual is: "These are the times! We are the people!" Next, my policy advisory work with UNDP in the 1990s and into the 21st century with the launch of the Millennium Development Goals (MDGs) in 2000, and implementing the initiative "Decentralizing the MDGs through Innovative Leadership (DMIL)" from 2002 to 2006.

Then after retiring from UNDP and launching in 2007 my consulting work as Innovative Leadership Services. Next in 2008 at NYU Wagner Graduate School of Public Service teaching "innovative leadership for sustainable human development" during the first of ten years of offering courses there. Finally, participating in and helping facilitate a State of the World Forum in Brazil in 2009 on "2020 Climate Leadership". There were of course other influences including Jean Houston's *Jump Time*, Ken Wilber's *Brief History of Everything*, James Hansen's climate research on catastrophic change, and the need for decisive action now, as found in the UN Intergovernmental Panel on Climate Change statement that "this is the defining moment", and many others.

In August 2009, I woke up concerning climate chaos, its dangers, and the *urgency* of taking radical measures of mitigation and adaptation. During my sixteen years in UNDP, I had known about global warming along with other crises facing humanity. But, it was in 2009 that I was seized by the realization that we were about to enter *the critical decade of 2010 – 2019* after which it might be too late. I became filled with resolve and energy to do what I could about climate chaos, ecocide, and the interconnected issues of misogyny, systemic poverty, plutocracy, racism, and perpetual war.

Thus began a decade of giving talks around the world, and lectures to my graduate students at NYU Wagner about multiple, interlocking crises, the opportunities of whole system transformation, and the role of the movement of movements (MoM), and innovative leadership. That decade was also when in 2013 I launched my blog, "A Compassionate Civilization", and published in 2017 a book by the same name, with the subtitle: *The Urgency of Sustainable Development and Mindful Activism.*

When I first thought of publishing these talks, it was primarily for the sake of documentation and knowledge sharing. The more I reread and reflected on them and the turbulent times in which we are living, the more I realized that publishing them now *can help empower and equip activists in the critical decade of 2020 – 2029 as a movement of movements (MoM) creating a world of ecological and human justice.* It was then that I knew that this has been one of my priorities for many years.

I gave these twelve talks commissioned by six organizations, between 2010 and 2019 in nine cities in five countries to over 3,000 people around the world. There are videos online of some of the talks. (See Appendix One for the URLs.) My UNDP decentralization, local governance, and urban development talks and papers and my NYU Wagner lectures are not included but are planned for other publications.

Taken as a whole, these twelve presentations and keynotes touch on several important topics. They focus on innovative leadership for sustainable development. They explore public service, and peace. They raise questions about what constitutes the social contract. They describe how ours is a critical time of crisis and opportunity. There is the need for sustainable, regenerative human development. A compassionate civilization is emerging even now. It is critical to develop in government, civil society, and business the skills and methods of innovative leadership including participatory facilitation, social artistry, integral thinking, and mindfulness. Transformative and collaborative leadership are key modalities. The institutional capacities to empower and engage citizens in participatory governance must be developed.

Global-local citizenship and lives of world service are needed. We must focus on community and organizational development. Integral, creative peace building is essential. And, we must develop strategies and partnerships as a movement of movements (MoM).

The Division of Public Administration and Development Management (DPADM) of the United Nations Department of Economic and Social Affairs (UNDESA) contracted four presentations (talks 3, 4, 6, 8) for their annual series of the UN Public Service Awards and Global Forum held in Tanzania, Bahrain, the Republic of Korea, and New York City. In addition to speaking, I often led a workshop, trained facilitators for breakout groups, and/or wrote a background paper.

The Institute of Cultural Affairs (ICA) International, and ICA Nepal asked me to give a keynote (5) in their global conference on human development held in Nepal. ICA USA asked me to give two talks (1 and 12) in their headquarters in Chicago.

The Building Creative Communities Conference (BCCC) commissioned two keynotes (2 and 11) for their annual events in Colquitt, Georgia. I also helped facilitate small group discussions.

Oklahoma City University (OCU) requested one keynote (7) at their creative peace-building symposium.

Horace Mann School (HMS) in New York City commissioned one special presentation (9) for students, faculty, administrators, and parents on global citizenship and world service. In addition, I facilitated a group workshop.

And finally, organizers of the World Fair Field and International Day of Peace Symposium requested a public presentation (10) for the citizens of Fairfield, Iowa, and students and faculty of local schools and universities. I also facilitated a small group discussion.

The talks were given in the cities and countries of Manama, Bahrain; Kathmandu, Nepal; Seoul, Republic of Korea; Dar es Salaam, Tanzania; New York City, New York; Chicago, Illinois; Oklahoma City, Oklahoma; Colquitt, Georgia; and Fairfield, Iowa. The participants of several of the conferences and events were from many countries around the world.

While reading, you may wish to imagine that you are sitting in that space, in that city, in that country, listening, thinking about, and deciding what you can do with these ideas, methods, and actions in your own life and work in our critical decade of 2020 – 2029.

The talks are arranged chronologically to allow the reader to experience the evolution of ideas and their expression for different purposes, audiences, and sponsors.

All twelve talks challenge the listener/reader to confront the multiple crises facing humanity. The first nine talks identify five crises, with the final three talks adding a sixth. All of the talks describe a vision, opportunities, pathways, or areas of transformation leading to a hoped-for future of a sustainable, just world. In the ninth talk, an emerging "compassionate" civilization is announced for the first time. Before that, it has been called a new or empathic civilization. Leadership methods needed are discussed in talks 2 – 4 and 8 – 12. These are described in various talks as innovative (2, 9), transformative (3), collaborative (8), facilitative (4, 10 – 12), creative (2, 4), integral (4, 9), and mindful/servant leadership (9). The second talk has the most detailed description of three types of innovative leadership including diagrams. Talks 10 and 11 describe six principles guiding the areas of transformation.

The movement of movements (MoM) is outlined in talks 9 – 12. Self-care is discussed in talks 10 and 11. Talk 1 lists the UN Millennium Development Goals (MDGs), mentions several former ICA staff and what they are doing in international development, and describes the role of ICA USA. ICA's Fifth City community development project, and UNDP's Local Initiative Facility in Urban Environment (LIFE), and the Decentralizing the MDGs through Innovative Leadership (DMIL) initiative are discussed in talks 2 and 3. The UN Sustainable Development Goals (SDGs) are found in talk 10. E-governance is highlighted in talk 6. An integral analysis and recommended actions related to war and peace are found in talk 7. Talks 1 and 3 include questions of social philosophy. Global citizenship is touched on in talk 9. Talk 12 shows how the ICA archival collections of methods and models can influence the MoM in its strategic work and in dealing with impediments (crises) in order to help move society toward a utopian vision rather than a dystopic one.

Following the twelve talks, an Epilogue shares reflection on our current critical decade of 2020 – 2029 beginning with the trauma and chaos of a viral pandemic, rising authoritarianism, racism, climate fires, economic collapse, and more. Then in Appendix Two, there are two additional talks that were given *before* the critical decade of 2010 – 2019 but contain relevant information. These presentations were made at ICA events, one in 1994 in Lonavala, India, at an ICAI global human development conference, and another in 1995 in Seattle, Washington, USA. They both cover whole system transformation, international development and the UN, sustainable human development, and the LIFE program. The talk in India touches on the new paradigm, social philosophy of humanness and development, the role of ICAI, and the work several former ICA staff were conducting with me as UNDP consultants. The Seattle talk goes into urbanization and touches on urban development.

You can read the chapters/speeches in whatever sequence you wish based on your interests of theme, sponsor, event, date, country, or other factors. If you decide to read them chronologically you will be able to see how ideas and their expression evolved over time and with different audiences and purposes. And if you want to read talks given before the critical decade of 2010 – 2019, go to Appendix Two.

As seen above, readers can expect to encounter some of the key concepts and methods several times as they read the book. This repetition can enhance learning and internalizing of and dialogue with the material in your own thinking and action. The reader will also see variations in the content and expression of themes.

In the back matter, you will find, in addition to acknowledgments, an appendix of the author's videos, podcasts, websites, social media sites, and books. There is also a bibliography of books and online sites related to this publication.

Many of the ideas and methods in these speeches found their way into my blog on a compassionate civilization begun in 2013 to the present, my 2017 book *A Compassionate*

Civilization: The Urgency of Sustainable Development and Mindful Activism – Reflections and Recommendations, and my lectures on innovative leadership for sustainable development given over ten years at New York University (NYU) Wagner Graduate School of Public Service. There was also a reverse relationship where my blog, book, and lectures influenced some of the later public talks.

The crises, principles, strategies, and methods identified in the book can act as guides for your own activism. Readers can take note of the use of questions, pauses for participant dialogue, diagrams, rituals, music, meditation, movement, poetry, and other techniques in many of the talks to facilitate and stimulate thought and interaction among participants. You may want to study and practice the effective leadership methods elaborated in the book: group facilitation, social artistry, integral thinking, mindfulness, and others. You may also wish to hold a book study group to explore the insights concerning sustainable development and the implications of other themes in the speeches. If you are a teacher, you can ask your students to study the content, methods, and/or style of delivery used in selected presentations. You can also share some of the talks with your networks and colleagues, share excerpts in your blog, podcast, or website, or use them to develop your own presentations, writing, planning, or training events.

May humanity move toward ecological, compassionate communities, organizations, networks, cities, nations, and planetary society through the commitment and passion of the movement of movements (MoM) making use of innovative leadership methods.

Participants in UN Global Forum 2013 in Bahrain UN Photo

Speaking at UN Global Forum in Bahrain UN Photo

TWELVE CALLS TO ACTION DURING
THE CRITICAL DECADE OF 2010 – 2019

World Fair Field 2018 participants during the interactive presentation

World Fair Field 2018 participants moving into action

1

"Preparing International Development Initiatives"

ICA USA Think Tank on International Initiatives

GreenRise, Chicago, Illinois, USA
27 March 2010

I deliver my first call to action.

From my memoir, Serving People & Planet: *"In March 2010, at the invitation of Dr. Terry Bergdall, CEO of ICA USA, I gave the keynote for an international development think tank held in Chicago at the ICA USA headquarters. I had not been there for many years and was excited to be back in Chicago and at the ICA with which I had loved working for 22 years before my UN days. I was nervous about speaking to my colleagues concerning my life and views; and I spoke much longer than my allotted time. There is a video on YouTube of my presentation.*

1

This was the first time that I declared in a public talk, outside of my NYU Wagner class lectures, that 'ours is the most critical decade and century in human history' because of ecological, social, economic, and political crises. My talk seemed to shock some of the colleagues but overall was well received. I continued in all of my following interventions to speak and write that message along with what we should do to respond to these systemic crises." (pages 179 – 180)

1. State of You and Me

Thanks to Terry Bergdall, CEO of ICA USA, for inviting me to set a context for your deliberations on international initiatives. It is good to see Dick Alton, Jan Sanders, and Bruce Williams here, and many other colleagues. It is wonderful to be here with people from ICA International, ICA USA, ICA Canada, ICA Nepal, ICA Bangladesh, and ICA UK. How are you doing? Or, as Larry Ward asked, what is your Jerusalem? Let us take a few minutes in silent meditation. (pause) Let me read something for you from *The Way of the Bodhisattva* written by Shantideva more than one thousand years ago. A bodhisattva is a person who vows to relieve the suffering of all beings.

May I be a guard for those who are protectorless,
A guide for those who journey on the road,
For those who wish to go across the water,
May I be a boat, a raft, a bridge.

May I be an isle for those who yearn for landfall,
And a lamp for those who long for light;

For those who need a resting place, a bed;
For all who need a servant, may I be their slave.

May I be the wishing jewel, the vase of plenty,
A word of power and the supreme healing;
May I be the tree of miracles,
And for every being the abundant cow.

Like the earth and the pervading elements,
Enduring as the sky itself endures,
For boundless multitude of living beings,
May I be their ground and sustenance.

Thus for everything that lives,
As far as are the limits of the sky,
May I provide their livelihood and nourishment
Until they pass beyond the bonds of suffering.
(pg. 51, 52, Shambhala 2003)

My stance from Christianity is one of humility, gratitude, and compassion. The future is indeed open. All is possible. From my Buddhist practice, I am committed to compassion and understanding, acknowledging suffering and relieving suffering. These are indeed the times, and we are the people.

Who are we? We are like a family. Yet, we have each changed. We do not know each other exactly anymore. We must honor the new us, ICAI newness, and ICA USA resurgence.

I spent twenty-two years with the ICA working at the grassroots project level (bottom up), representing an NGO, and a global, secular-religious, experimental family order. I helped take the Order Ecumenical out of being in 1988 in Caracas. We sent ourselves out to join the "larger order" or movement to leaven the world; since then we have done much. ICA became one NGO among many. I was last in Chicago twenty-five years ago. In 1990, I left ICA Venezuela to the Venezuelans and moved back to USA, to New York City, with $900 in my bank account and a family of four with no place to live and no job or income. And yet, I was completely fearless. I first worked with the Mega Cities Project at NYU at the invitation of George Walters. From there, I met Dr. Shabbir Cheema at UNDP who hired me as a consultant, and later I became a UNDP policy adviser.

I worked sixteen years with UNDP at the global policy level (top down), representing the UN. When Mary and I first walked into the UN we saw "ICA International" written on one of the walls in an exhibit of NGOs with ECOSOC consultative status. I was excited to receive a UN passport; I felt like a global citizen. I was last at an ICAI gathering six years ago in Lonavala, India, as a UNDP policy adviser. I have also been on the ICAI Advisory Board. I involved Jan Sanders, Gary Forbes, John Oyler, and others in UNDP work as consultants. I helped introduce ICA methods, social artistry, and emotional intelligence to UNDP. I designed and coordinated the Local Initiative Facility for Urban Environment (LIFE) program, the Decentralized Governance Program, the Decentralizing the Millennium Development Goals (MDGs) through Innovative Leadership (DMIL), launched a community of practice on decentralized governance (CoP), conducted research, prepared publications, and collaborated with Jean Houston in DMIL.

In 2006, I retired as principal policy advisor on decentralization, local governance and urban development and we held a "Dance of Life" celebration for my UNDP retirement.

Then for the past four years, it has been "just me" as founder of Innovative Leadership Services, working and being where I am called. After thirty-eight years representing two organizations (ICA and UNDP), now I am doing what I choose each day. I have been consulting with UNDP, UNDESA, the East-West Center, and teaching at NYU and Columbia University. I became a newlywed, and a first-time grandfather. Thank you again for the invitation to be here together with you, breathing, thinking, hoping, loving.

2. State of the World
We have just entered the most critical decade in human history, a time to do or die. Other times thought they were it; they were wrong. This is it. We are amidst a whole system transformation – a time of chaos, crisis, and possibility. We are facing multiple, interlocking crises of HIV/AIDS, gender inequality, increasing poverty, failed governance, unsustainable energy, and climate chaos. We have the tools and technology needed but not the collective will to action. We must at one and the same time transform individual consciousness and behavior and collective culture and systems.

This crisis is an opportunity to reinvent human society from the bottom up and the top down based on principles of justice, equity, sustainability, and participation.

Some of the interlocking crises and opportunities include:

Environmental: This is the end of a civilization. We must invent a new civilization based on principles of sustainability, justice, equity, and participation. Global warming is real: there is melting of ice in Greenland, the Arctic, and mountain glaciers (Himalayas, Andes, etc.); temperatures are warming; sea rise is happening; there is flooding of coastal cities and islands; desertification, droughts and food collapse are taking place; there are mega storms; a massive die-back of species is taking place; social, political, and economic chaos is increasing. This crisis has accelerated over the past fifty years of fossil fuel industrialization – my/our generation. There is a water crisis. In 2014, we may have Peak Oil and the collapse will accelerate. The next ten years will tell the story of our future – misery or happiness. The opportunity is that we can invent sustainable development on this planet.

Economic: The crisis is a financial system divorced from nature and social justice. The opportunity is that of inventing a new financial order, reinventing money, reinvesting value in nature and people, and ending the madness of the ever-accelerating consumption-production cycle.

Political: There is governance collapse and a crisis of a democracy controlled by corporations. The opportunity is of reinventing governance that is participatory, just, and in line with sustainable development.

Social: There is a crisis in health care and education. The opportunity is of catalyzing a new common sense of the universal right of education and health care.

Cultural: The crisis is the sunset-effect of fear-based fundamentalisms. The opportunity is to shift to global, empathic consciousness (Jeremy Rifkin) with the rise of the cultural creatives (Paul Ray).

There is a pathway forward. We must end the ever-increasing production-consumption society. We must put an end to unlimited growth. We must create a sustainable, equitable, participatory, just society, with renewable energy, a just financial system, participatory governance, and environmental protection of water, air, soil, plants, and animals.

There is a need for new thinking, new assumptions, new myths, new policies, and new collective action.

Awakenment is primary to engagement. How to stay awake? How to act mindfully?

We need a "lure of becoming", as Jean Houston calls it, that draws us out of the present delusion and morass toward a compelling, hoped-for future.

3. **State of International Development**
The two questions we must ask everyone are: 1) What is a human being? and 2) What is development?

History of International Development: Human beings have been developing for 50,000, 200,000, 2 million years. International development as a profession is very recent, only 65 years old, my age, the age of the UN. In the beginning, the focus of international development was economic development, then socio-economic development, then socio-political-cultural-economic-environmental development, then holistic human development, and now integral development.

There is a myth of development, that it comes from the outside and emulates the so-called developed nations. There is also a myth of progress, that improvements in living standards are inevitable and unending. Fortunately, there is now a Gross National Happiness index to challenge the limited Gross National Product (GNP) index. We can bring an end to the exclusive focus on the production-consumption cycle and paradigm.

Aspects of international development intervention include the actors and issues. Actors of development intervention include multilateral organizations (the UN, World Bank, etc.) and bilateral organizations (national government organizations assisting developing countries). National, state, and city governments, and cities associations are key actors. Nongovernmental organizations (NGOs) and community-based organizations (CBOs) are other key actors. The private sector is a powerful actor. Some would say that corporations already rule the world. Then, there is academia, and media, often controlled by power elites.

Issues of development intervention include HIV/AIDS, governance, leadership, participation, human rights, electoral reform, judicial reform, e-governance, information technology, decentralization, local governance, urban development, rural development, public administration, poverty eradication/promotion of equity, gender equality/women's empowerment, helping in crisis situations/ conflict/ dispute resolution, responding to natural disasters, dealing with environmental issues/global warming/and promoting green energy, caring for children/youth, dealing with food security, promoting education, and health, and dealing with failed states.

In development epistemology, we ask what is real? What can we know? How do we know what we know? It can be through statistics but also through anecdotes and personal perceptions.

The Millennium Development Goals (MDGs) are eight goals to be achieved by 2015 that respond to the world's main development challenges. The MDGs are drawn from the actions and targets contained in the Millennium Declaration that was adopted by 189 nations and signed by 147 heads of state and governments during the UN Millennium Summit in September 2000.

The eight MDGs break down into 21 quantifiable targets that are measured by 60 indicators. The eight goals are to: 1) eradicate extreme poverty and hunger; 2) achieve universal primary education; 3) promote gender equality and empower women; 4) reduce child mortality; 5) improve maternal health; 6) combat HIV/AIDS, malaria and other diseases; 7) ensure environmental sustainability; and 8) develop a Global Partnership for Development.

The MDGs synthesize, in a single package, many of the most important commitments made separately at the international conferences and summits of the 1990s. They recognize explicitly the interdependence between growth, poverty reduction, and sustainable development. They acknowledge that development rests on the foundations of democratic governance, the rule of law, respect for human rights, peace, and security. They are based on time-bound and measurable targets accompanied by indicators for monitoring progress. They bring together, in the eighth goal, the responsibilities of developing countries with those of developed countries. They are founded on a global partnership that was endorsed at the International Conference on Financing for Development in Monterrey, Mexico, in March 2002, and again at the Johannesburg World Summit on Sustainable Development in August 2002.

Levels of development intervention can be the individual, family, community, organization, institution, system, city, state, nation, region, and globe.

Forms of development intervention can be projects, demonstrations, programs, impact, service systems, policy and institutional arrangements, advocacy, administration and management, fund raising, public relations, campaigns and awareness raising, Communities of Practice, and networks and interchange.

Geography of development interventions can be in Africa, Asia/ Pacific, Latin America/Caribbean, Eastern Europe/Commonwealth of Independent States (CIS), the Arab States, Western Europe, and North America.

Cycles of development interventions include strategic and situational analysis, design of intervention/planning, design of indicators, funding/staffing, training, initiation of intervention, management, implementation, monitoring, evaluation, documentation, and feed back.

Methods of development interventions include ICA's Technology of Participation (ToP), Jean Houston's social artistry processes, Ken Wilber's integral approach, Emotional Intelligence, Appreciative Inquiry, Open Space, Whole System Design, and many others.

4. **State of ICA USA**

How can we inspire ourselves to do the greatest work that we can do?

Issues and questions center around the role of ICAI, the role of ICA USA and other national ICAs, funding (foundations, corporations, government, individuals), staffing (who? paid? volunteers?), coordination, methods (beyond ToP), strategic priorities (themes? geography?), allies, and measurement of impact.

We need to do a SWOT analysis on ICA's international development work:

Strengths: new CEO; Kemper building; track record; ToP; archives; volunteers; and spirit.

Weaknesses: few staff; few funds; and unclear strategy.

Opportunities: ICA former staff are already doing international work: literacy projects in India, Rwanda and North America (Elise Packard); ICA Japan's international development work in Chile, Haiti, Philippines, India, Kenya, Vietnam, Tanzania, Mexico, and Indonesia (Wayne Ellsworth and Shizuyo Sato); ICA Canada's work in Africa (Listen to the Drumming in Zambia, Kenya, Togo, Ghana, Tanzania, and Rwanda); ICA Nepal's Social Artistry work (Tatwa Timsina, and Jan Sanders); HIV/AIDS work in Africa Self Help Groups (Louise Singleton, Dick Alton, Bruce Williams); national ICA's (ICA Zimbabwe and Rotary 3H grant for self help groups of women); Sherwood and Eunice Shankland's work with the UN's Food and Agriculture Organization (FAO); Abby North's work in Africa on HIV/AIDS mitigation; ICA International's advocacy work on forestry and a global conference planned in 2012 in Nepal; providing funding support for initiatives; ICA Taiwan's work with the International Association of Facilitators (IAF) community outreach in Asia and leadership training for the UN; ICA Peru's willingness to work on disaster relief and recovery; influencing USA government policy and support internationally; Association of Rural Development (ARD) (Kenn Ellison, Gary Forbes); Education – Bruce Williams; and Leadership Inc. in China, Mongolia (Water and Health Advocacy Forum). My work as Innovative Leadership Services has included: working with UNDP as a consultant on urban development, with UNDESA on participatory methods, with governance capacity building and an Arab leadership network, consulting with the East-West Center on civil society leadership and sustainable development and governance, teaching at New York University Wagner on innovative leadership for human development, and localizing the MDGs in Asia.

Threats: thinking small and local only; not dealing with USA policies on climate change, etc.

Closing:
Some recommendations for ICA in its international development work include: be catalytic, leverage the greatest changes; work at various levels; advocate for policy change; think big; be bold; form partnerships with others – individuals and organizations; let go of taking credit for success; work in the US 90% of the time because the US is a major global contradiction; use new methods – Social Artistry, Emotional Intelligence, and Wilber's Quadrants; strengthen ICAI; and

use strategic priorities related to themes, and geography; and measure impacts.

These indeed are times of crisis. Are we the people to heed the call? The need is dramatically apparent. The resources are present; trillions of dollars are sloshing around the globe looking for good ideas and projects. We must think big, not just tinker. What is the grand strategy? Who are our allies? How to access resources? How to leave a legacy that moves forward for the next 100 years?

Where do we each put our life?

Our colleague Nelson Stover put it this way in his 2005 poem:

What Planet Earth needs now
Is a global organization of people
Committed – through their thinking, acting and passion –
To building a world based on:
Inclusive Profound Spirituality,
Participatory Social Processes and
Enhancing Ecological Practices.

2

"The Task Before Us Now"

Keynote Address for the 5th Building Creative Communities Conference

Cotton Hall, Colquitt, Georgia, USA
4 February 2011

*L*ess than a year after the first "critical decade" presentation in Chicago, I made my second call to action.

From Serving People & Planet: *"In early February, Bonnie led a beautiful water ceremony, and I gave a keynote address at the Building Creative Communities Conference (BC3) in Colquitt, Georgia. This was at the invitation of an ICA and social artistry colleague Joy Jinks, one of the organizers of the conference and a long-standing leader of her community. Years before, she and her daughter had been short-term volunteers in an ICA village project in Jamaica where I was codirector. It was good to see Jan Sanders, who was teaching social artistry at the conference. Colquitt is*

15

famous for its Swamp Gravy theater performances based on
community stories and performed each year in Cotton Hall
by community residents young and old. All around the small
town are huge, stunning murals depicting community stories
and values. Every year, Colquitt invited community leaders
from around the area and the country to come for training
in social artistry and community building.

"My talk challenged the participants to respond to this time
of crisis and opportunity by building an empathic society, com-
munity by community. I shared a number of stories and leader-
ship methods that they could make use of. After my keynote,
the Story Bridge founder Dr. Richard Geer took over and led
the group in sharing stories, and creating and performing a
play-in-a-day. It was incredible how this process built trust and
released energy for creative community building. I was sold on
the process and on Colquitt." (page 182)

Introduction:

Wasn't that the most incredible performance last night?!
After so many years of hearing about Swamp Gravy, at long
last I have been initiated into its mysteries! Thank you, Joy
Jinks, for inviting me and for your vision and commitment
over the years to empowering local communities.

I am delighted to be with each of you this week – those
from Florida State University, from local communities in
nine states and from the Jean Houston Foundation's social
artistry contingent. I accepted Joy's invitation because I
believe that you and I have been called here to do something extraordinary at this moment in history and evolution.

The great French paleontologist, priest, and theologian, Pierre Teilhard de Chardin wrote: "The task before us now, if we would not perish, is to shake off our ancient prejudices, and to build the Earth." (point to the Earth flag behind). I would like to add a few words to his quote: "The task before us now, in this most critical decade, if we would not perish, is to shake off our ancient prejudices, and to build the Earth, community by community, as innovative, creative leaders."

We are here for four days in the world-famous town of Colquitt to embody the Fifth Building Creative Communities Conference. We will be working in three areas: story telling, community development, and the art of social change or social artistry.

We will be performing for each other, learning from each other, and challenging and encouraging each other to be all that we can be. We are here on behalf of many, many people: our local communities, home states, our nation, planetary society, and all forms of life on this most beautiful planet of which we are aware, Earth. (point to Earth flag again)

I would invite us to think together over the next 50 minutes about four things: We are in "The Critical Decade" in which A New Civilization Is Emerging, which We Must Build Together Community by Community, utilizing Innovative, Creative Leadership.

First a bit about how you and I are already connected:

For you Southerners, some of my ancestors hail from Kentucky; Houston, Texas, is my birth place; I grew up in Oklahoma and went to undergraduate school there; and Asheville, North Carolina, is where I live half of each year.

For you community developers and those interested in NGOs, for the first 22 years of my professional life I was a national and regional executive-director of an NGO, the Institute of Cultural Affairs (ICA), conducting community, leadership, and organizational development in Asia, the Caribbean, and Latin America (Jamaica is where I first met Joy when she and her daughter volunteered with our community development project.) With the ICA, I learned that symbol and story are keys to community development.

For those interested in the UN or urban development, I was with the United Nations Development Programme (UNDP) for 16 years as principal policy advisor for decentralization, local governance, and urban development. With UNDP, I learned the importance of policy and institutional arrangements.

For you social artists, I have studied social artistry and human potential development with Jean Houston for 25 years and invited her to work with me at UNDP on decentralizing the eight Millennium Development Goals (MDGs) through innovative leadership. From Jean, I learned to mythologize not pathologize.

And for those interested in higher education or leadership, for the past four years I have been a New York University (NYU) professor in the Wagner Graduate School of Public Service and Director of Innovative Leadership Services doing facilitation and writing for the UN and other international organizations. I am learning that I am still driven to change the world and to continue to change myself.

(Please turn to a person near you and in one minute each share one crisis that is happening in the world.)

1. *The Critical Decade:*

I believe that we have just entered **the most critical decade** in human history – a time to do what is needful or face the direst of consequences. Other generations thought they were it; they were wrong; this is it. If we do the right things, the future of life on Earth can be brighter than we can imagine. If we do not, the future will be dismal and even disastrous.

We are amidst a whole systems transformation – a time of chaos, crisis, and possibility. We are facing multiple, interlocking crises including climate chaos, increasing poverty, failed governance, unsustainable energy, gender inequality, and an HIV/AIDS pandemic. Each of these crises, however, is also an unparalleled opportunity for reinvention.

We have the tools and technology needed to solve each of these crises, but we lack the collective agreement and will to action. We must, at the same time, transform individual consciousness and behavior and collective culture and systems.

These crises are an opportunity to reinvent nothing less than human society itself from the bottom up and the top down based on principles of sustainability, equity, justice, and participation. We can literally create a world that works for everyone – societies that enable each person to realize her or his full potential.

There are several interlocking crises which represent incredible opportunities:

Environmental –
Earth's natural systems that have supported human civilization for the past 12,000 years are changing drastically and
human societies will have to change quickly or adapt to a
diminished Earth over the long term. Global warming is real.
The Greenland ice cap is melting. Antarctica which has 90
percent of the earth's ice is melting; mountain glaciers in the
Andes and Himalayas are melting. Deforestation is accelerating. Carbon dioxide and methane gases are rapidly heating up
the planet. We are already past 350 parts per million (ppm)
of carbon dioxide in the atmosphere – the highest concentration without heating up the Earth. This means that the seas
will rise six feet and flood coastal cities and islands. In other
parts of the world, there will be massive desertification,
droughts, and food collapse. Mega storms will be the norm.
There is already a massive die-back of species. There will be
social, political, and economic crises with mass migration and
resource wars. Drinking water will become very scarce and
wars will be fought over this life-essential resource. The next
ten years will tell the story of our future – misery or happiness.

The opportunity before us is to let go of carbon-based
energy, death-energy, and to invent a sustainable development path for humanity.

We can shift to renewal energy, life-energy, from the sun,
water, wind, and ground heat. But, we must do this swiftly to
avert disaster.

Economic
The economic crisis we are in is a result of a financial system that is divorced from nature and social justice. The

opportunity here is to invent a new financial order, to reinvent money, and reinvest value in nature and people. And we
must end the madness of the consumption-production cycle.

Political
We are in a governance collapse. It is a crisis of democracy
which has become a plutocracy controlled by banks, other
corporations, and the super-rich. The opportunity lies in
reinventing governance that is participatory, just, and in line
with sustainable development goals.

Social
The major crises are in healthcare and education. We have
an opportunity to catalyze a new commonsense of the universal right to education and healthcare.

Cultural
We face a crisis of the sunset effect of fear-based fundamen-
talisms – Christian and Hindu as well as Muslim. Yet through
this, the opportunity exists with a shift to an evolutionary
Earth story, empathic consciousness, and the rise of the
Cultural Creatives (Paul Ray).

There is a pathway forward. We need to put an end to our
purely production-consumption society, end the unrealistic
concept of unlimited growth, and drive towards a sustainable, equitable, participatory, just society. We need renewable energy, an equitable financial system, participatory
governance, environmental protection, universal healthcare,
education for all, and gender equality. We need new thinking, new assumptions, and new myths, policies, and collective

action. Awakenment is primary to engagement. We need to understand how to stay awake and how to act mindfully. We need a Lure of Becoming, as Jean Houston calls it, that draws us out of the present delusions and morass toward a hoped-for future.

(Please turn to someone near you and share in one minute each where you see a sign however small of the emergence of a new civilization.)

2. *Emergence of a New Civilization:*
Within this moment of crisis, a **new civilization** is emerging. It is an Earth-based civilization of sustainable human development. In this new civilization, people will embody a consciousness of being part of the living Earth, of being part of the life force of our beautiful planet. We are Earthlings. All people and all life forms are our brothers and sisters. We have a common future or no future at all. People will embody behavior that is empathic and compassionate. People will embody a culture of peace, creativity, and learning. People will embody systems, policies and institutions of equality, justice, and universal participation in decision making. And, if we do not create such a civilization, the alternative is chaos, tyranny, suffering, and systems collapse.

(Please turn to someone near you and share in one minute each a key insight for you of effective community development.)

3. *Community by Community:*
In this critical decade, we must build the new civilization of sustainable human development **community by community**.

You are part of this conference because you know the importance of community level transformation. I would like to
share with you a few of my experiences in working to build a
new civilization community by community.

My first experiences in community development were on
the West Side of Chicago in the African-American ghetto in
the 1960s. The NGO that I was part of was catalyzing a demonstration of how any community in the world could transform itself economically, socially, culturally, and politically.
We called our pilot project 5th City. As people from outside
the community, our role was to empower, train, equip, and
connect the residents to do their own development.

We worked within a geographically delimited area and
involved all the people, all age groups, and addressed all
issues simultaneously. We called this integrated human
development. And, we found through hard experience that
culture and symbol were the keys to community renewal. 5th
City created songs, stories, and symbols that inspired residents to transform their community. There was a sculpture
of the Iron Human on 5th Avenue, songs of empowerment
in the preschool and in community meetings and stories
of heroes doing the impossible and creating a new world.
Residents understood that what they were doing was on
behalf of the whole world. 5th City was a global human development demonstration project, and this was perhaps the
most powerful motivation of all.

And, we learned that every community has a depth contradiction that is blocking its development that must be
addressed. For 5th City it was the victim image – people felt

that they were powerless to create their own destiny. One way to counter this was to create empowering songs for the pre school children. One song goes like this (use movements): "I am always falling down. But I know what I can do. I can pick myself up and say to myself. I'm the greatest too. It doesn't matter if you're big or small. You live now if you live at all. I am always falling down. But I know what I can do."

Based on the 5th City model, we created a participatory planning methodology that any community could use. We took it around the world and launched human development projects in the 24 time zones of the planet. I helped launch two projects in the Republic of Korea, one on Cheju Island in the village of Kwang Yung Il Ri and one near the DMZ, Kuh Du I Ri. I also worked in village projects in Jamaica (Woburn Lawn) and Venezuela (Cano Negro). Eventually our NGO was working in hundreds of communities around the world including mass replication in India and Kenya.

Then, when I joined UNDP in 1990, I helped design and launch a global program to renew urban slums and squatter settlements around the world. I started the LIFE program (the Local Initiative Facility for the Urban Environment) in 12 pilot countries around the world. We worked in 300 cities and raised $15 million dollars. Residents worked in collaboration with the local authorities and NGOs in improving their living environment. We called this "local-local dialogue." Through small grants for micro projects the local people improved their solid waste management, potable water, environmental health and education, and drainage, gender equality, and created local jobs.

At the beginning of this century, the nations of the world launched through the UN the Millennium Development Goals (MDGs) initiative. This was the first time in history that the world had agreed on tangible, time bound goals to improve the lives of people all around the world. These goals included eradicating poverty, empowering women, providing early education, protecting the environment, and mitigating HIV/AIDS and malaria. Many of us in the UN believed that the key to achieving these goals was in their localization. Therefore, we launched initiatives to localize the MDGs in local communities around the world – one that I launched – Decentralizing the MDGs through Innovative Leadership - I will talk about in a minute.

And, the Swamp Gravy/Building Creative Communities movement is an important effort to create a new civilization community by community, story by story. We are here to advance that cause.

(Please turn to someone near you and in one minute each share a method of creative leadership that you are aware of.)

4. *Employing Innovative, Creative Leadership:*
What are the most effective means in this critical decade with which to build a new civilization community by community? I have found that **innovative, creative leadership** approaches are an essential key to unlock the potential of communities and organizations. From four decades of international work I brought together several leadership methods that I offer through Innovative Leadership Services including my course at New York University Wagner Graduate School

of Public Services, and in my facilitation and writing for the UN and other international organizations. I would like to offer you a few of the many effective ways of building creative communities through creative leadership.

Change requires new systems, policies, and institutions but these are not enough. To create effective change, we must also transform individual consciousness and behavior, and collective culture. These four dimensions of leadership based on Ken Wilber's quadrants of integral development are all essential: change that is both individual and collective and internal and external. (Draw the quadrants.)

Within each of these quadrants of leadership, we must work on four levels of transformation: physical/sensory, psychological/historic, mythic/symbolic, and unitive/spiritual. These four levels as delineated by Jean Houston in her social artistry work are all essential for effective change to take place. Swamp Gravy itself is working powerfully in the cultural quadrant and at the mythic level.

The third set of methods that is part of innovative leadership is the Technology of Participation or ToP. This array of effective leadership methods was developed by the Institute of Cultural Affairs (ICA) with which I worked for 21 years. ToP includes, among others, methods of effective group conversations, group workshops, and strategic planning.

The ORID group conversation method takes people on a journey from Observation (what do you see?), to Reflection (what does this remind you of?), to Interpretation (what does this mean to you?), and finally to their <u>D</u>ecisions (what are you going to do about it?) concerning what to do. The ToP workshop method includes setting the stage, brainstorming, grouping of data, naming of clusters of data, and reflecting on the group's consensus. The ToP strategic planning method, using the workshop method for each step, enables a community or organization to articulate their vision of their hoped for future, analyze what could block or enable that vision, create broad strategic directions to achieve the vision, identify tactical systems to achieve the strategies, and decide what discrete actions or "implementaries" in what timeframe will do the job.

These are three sets of innovative leadership methods that I teach in my graduate courses at NYU Wagner and use in my consulting with the UN, etc. And they work!

As we work together today and tomorrow, I would invite us to make use of the most creative leadership methods and approaches that we know or can invent.

Conclusion:

We are now going into our three tracks: story telling, community development, and tomorrow, the art of social change or social artistry. Our challenge is to remember that we are in the most critical decade in human history, that we are creating nothing less than a new civilization, that we are building that civilization community by community, and that we are making use of the most creative, innovative leadership approaches and methods that we can access.

My sincere hope and belief are that each track and each of us individually will experience creative breakthroughs of self understanding and expression, cultural creativity, and systemic reinvention during the next three days. The time, space, energy, and insight that we have is sufficient for that to happen.

My challenges to the three tracks are:

Storytelling: As you tell the stories of a local community, how can you dramatize this critical moment in history, the emerging new civilization, and the necessity of community development and creative leadership?

Community Development: How can you help a local community respond creatively to the environmental (lower carbon foot print), economic (jobs), social (health and education), political (local governance), and cultural (diversity and compassion) crises that face it?

Art of Social Change: How can you use innovative, creative leadership approaches to enliven and deepen societal transformation?

(Please turn to someone near you and share in one minute each one of your questions or comments. Now, who heard an amazing question or comment from your neighbor? Please share that with all of us.)

To close, please repeat after me the adapted Teilhard de Chardin quote:

"The task before us now,
in this most critical decade,
if we would not perish,
is to shake off our ancient prejudices,
and to build a new Earth civilization,
community by community,
as innovative, creative leaders."

3

"Transformative Leadership for Sustainable Human Development"

UN Africa and Global Public Service Awards and Global Forum

Dar es Salaam, United Republic of Tanzania 20 – 23 June 2011

*T*hree months after the call to action in Colquitt, Georgia, USA, I traveled to Tanzania at the invitation of the UN to give my third "critical decade" talk to a group gathered from around the world for a UN Africa/Global forum. The theme of the forum was "Transformative Leadership in Public Administration and Innovation in Governance: Creating a Better Life for All."

From Serving People & Planet: "In mid-June, I flew to Dar es Salam, Tanzania. On the way to Mother Africa, the birthplace of the human race, I asked myself: What can I give to Africa and to planet Earth? How can I give voice to the voiceless, to future generations, to the waters, air, soil, plants and animals, and to the poor? Flying over Greece, I thought about its lost grandeur, and wondered if that was a symbol of the future collapse of Western civilization. I found myself thinking about my grandchildren, Phoenix and Mariela. Then, we flew across the Sahara desert just west of the Red Sea, then west of Addis Ababa, remembering that I was first there in 1969, just married, 25 years old.

"While in Dar, I gave a keynote address at the UN Public Service Day Awards and Global Forum and facilitated a workshop. Before the forum I had prepared a background paper and trained facilitators. The organizers had given each participant and speaker a colorful batik printed cloth with the UN logo on it. When I gave my keynote, I draped the cloth around one shoulder. Dr. Adriana Alberti of UNDESA had kindly invited me to do this consultancy. It was good to be back in Dar since the time I was there with UNDP several years prior." (pages 183 – 184)

Below is my prepared statement. My talk was a shorter version and began: "Jambo! Habari? [a Swahili greeting] I am very happy to be with you. Why are we here – in Africa, in this gathering? I have returned to Mother Africa, East Africa, as a pilgrimage to the birthplace of the human species. I am part of this gathering because I am convinced that you and I can make a difference in this glorious, suffering world by what we think, say and do. Why are you here? (Turn to a person near you and share in one minute each why you are here.)"

Introduction

The aim of this keynote is to provide the UN Public Service Awards and Global Forum 2011 with a reflection on the critical times in which we live, the substantive integration and purpose of the Forum workshops and future scenarios of development, governance and leadership. First, there will be a brief reflection on social philosophy and the social contract raising a few important questions. Next, there will be an analysis of the critical decade of crisis and opportunity in which we find ourselves, the new civilization that is emerging and the importance of working at the community level. Following this, there is a discussion of the role of transformational leadership in 21st century public service. Finally, I will provide a few thoughts on the integration of the themes of the four Forum workshops and some of the possible follow up actions to the conference. The talk includes the personal and professional reflections and experiences of the author.

I.   Social Philosophy

What is a *human* being? What is development? What then is human development? What is the purpose of societal organization and governance in relation to human development?

These are not only philosophical questions but urgent, practical questions. These are some of the profound questions facing us as a species. Our responses to these questions, both in our individual thought and behavior and in our collective culture and systems, will determine how human society and life itself flourishes or declines on planet Earth. If this is so, how is it so?

There are many views of what constitutes a human being. Is a human being a spiritual being of infinite worth? Or, primarily a consumer of goods and services? Or, a resource for economic production? Or, primarily a citizen of the State? Or, simply another mammal? Or, a child of God? Is a human being basically good? Or, fundamentally evil? Does each human being who is born have universal rights guaranteed by society? What are the rights of future generations? What is the full potential of each human being? What is the ultimate purpose of human beings on planet Earth or in the universe as a whole? Our answers to these questions spring from our own acculturation and socialization as provided by our culture, religion, political ideology, personal reflection, age, sex, and so forth. Some people believe that only their group is truly human and that all others lack truth and legitimacy.

The dominant answer in the world today to the question of what constitutes development is material and economic progress, industrialization, and modernization. The race is on to increase GDP per capital and fuel a consumption-production society at any cost to nature and people. However, this purely economic definition is doing much harm to natural systems and human culture.

Each definition of humanness carries with it an implicit or explicit definition of development. If a human being is primarily a spiritual being, then society would be designed in a way that would help each person realize his/her spiritual potential. If a human being is primarily a consumer, then he/she is to be manipulated by advertisements to purchase certain goods and services. If a human being is primarily a citizen of a democratic state, then she/he is empowered to express her/his opinions through voting and is responsible to act in accord with the laws of the State. If a human being is understood simply as another mammal, then she/he will be treated that way. If a human being is understood to be a child of God, then she/he will be cherished as a holy being.

If a human being is understood to be basically good, then society structures itself to nurture this quality and will design systems based on trust of this basic goodness. If a human being is understood as fundamentally evil, then society will design systems that seek to control and punish these dark impulses. If every human being who is born has universal human rights, then society will design systems to ensure adequate opportunities and access to quality education, healthcare, housing, credit, and self expression of each person. If future generations have the same rights as the present generation, then society will ensure that the resources of the Earth are preserved and developed. If every human being has the right to realize his/her full potential in this life, then society will be designed to ensure that this can happen. If human beings believe that they have an ultimate purpose on planet Earth and in the universe, then this will provoke profound dialogue in society and help direct the design of social systems toward a learning society.

What then is "human development"? As we have seen, different definitions will flow from different views of the human being. In the view of the United Nations and the international community at large, the human being is guaranteed universal rights by society as articulated in the Declaration of Human

Rights. The UN has been analyzing and promoting "human development" or "sustainable human development" over the past twenty years. Furthermore, the eight Millennium Development Goals (MDGs) were agreed upon to provide tangible targets for human development over the short term.

How then do nations and local communities understand the *social compact* that guides the design of social systems for the benefit of all human beings, all living beings, and the finite resources of planet Earth, including plants, animals, water, soil, and air? Based on the Universal Declaration of Human Rights, the social compact directs that human beings agree to care for each other to ensure that each person has the necessary conditions for a full and meaningful life while ensuring that future generations have the same right.

This means that for all people to enjoy these rights, no group of individuals should be allowed to make this impossible by the over accumulation of economic wealth, political power, or cultural dominance.

With this reflection as a backdrop, what are the current challenges facing humanity and indeed all life on Earth?

II. **The Critical Decade: Crisis and Opportunity**

Many social analysts, the author included, believe that we have just entered **the most critical decade** in human history — a time to do what is needful or face the direst of consequences. Other generations thought they were it; they were wrong; this is it. If we do the right things, the future of life on Earth can be brighter than we can imagine. If we do not, the future could be dismal and even disastrous.

We are in a whole systems transformation – a time of chaos, crisis, and possibility. We are facing multiple, inter-locking crises including climate chaos, economic injustice, increasing poverty, dysfunctional governance, unsustainable energy, gender inequality, and an HIV/AIDS pandemic. Each of these crises, however, is also an unparalleled opportunity for reinvention of the human enterprise.

We as a global society have the tools and technology needed to solve each of these crises; what we lack is col-lective agreement and action. We must, at the same time, transform individual consciousness and behavior and collec-tive culture and systems.

These crises are an opportunity to reinvent nothing less than human society itself from the bottom up, the top down and the inside out based on principles of *sustainabil-ity, equity, justice, and participation*. We can literally create a world that works for everyone – societies that enable each person to realize her or his full potential.

There are several interlocking crises which represent incredible opportunities:

Environmental
The natural systems of Earth that have supported human civilization for the past 12,000 years are changing drastically and human societies must adjust quickly or adapt to a dimin-ished Earth over the long term. Global climate change is real. The Greenland ice cap is melting. Antarctica which has 90 percent of the earth's ice is melting. Mountain glaciers in the Andes and Himalayas and the Siberian permafrost are

melting. Deforestation is accelerating. Carbon dioxide and methane gases are rapidly heating up the planet. We are already past 350 parts per million (ppm) of carbon dioxide in the atmosphere – the highest concentration without dangerously heating up the Earth. This means that if this heating up goes unabated, the seas will rise six feet and flood coastal cities and cover islands. In other parts of the world, there will be massive desertification, droughts, and food collapse. Mega storms will be the norm. There is already a massive die-back of species. There will be social, political, and economic crises with mass migration and resource wars. Drinking water will become very scarce and wars will be fought over this life-essential resource. The next ten years will tell the story of our future – misery or happiness.

The opportunity before us is to let go of carbon-based energy, "death-energy" from dead animals and plants, and to invent a sustainable development path for humanity and all life forms. We can and must shift to renewal energy, "life-energy", from the sun, water, wind, geo-thermal, and algae. But, we must do this swiftly to avert disaster.

Economic
The global economic crisis we are in is a result of a financial system that is divorced from nature and social justice. Corporations, treated as persons and driven solely by profit motive, are endangering natural ecosystems, and subverting democratic institutions. The opportunity here is to invent a new financial order, to reinvent money, and reinvest value in nature and people. And we must end the madness of

the consumption-production cycle and create the Learning Society.

Political

We are experiencing governance collapse. It is a crisis of democracies which have become plutocracies controlled by banks and insurance companies, the oil and coal industry, pharmaceutical companies, other corporations, and the super-rich. The opportunity lies in reinventing governance that is participatory, just and in line with sustainable development goals.

Social

The major crises are in healthcare and education. We have an opportunity to catalyze a new commonsense of the universal rights to education and healthcare.

Cultural

We face a crisis of the sunset effect of fear-based fundamentalisms – Christian and Hindu as well as Muslim. Yet through this, the opportunity exists for a shift to an evolutionary Earth story, empathic consciousness, and the rise of the Cultural Creatives (Paul Ray).

There is a pathway forward. We need to put an end to our purely production-consumption society, end the unrealistic concept of unlimited growth and drive towards a sustainable, equitable, participatory, just society. We need renewable energy, an equitable financial system, participatory governance, environmental protection, universal healthcare, education for all, and gender equality. We need new ways of thinking, new assumptions, and new myths, policies, and collective action. Awakenment must proceed and accompany action and commitment. We need to understand how to stay awake and how to act mindfully. We need a "lure of becoming" that draws us out of the present delusion and morass toward a hoped-for future.

Within this very moment of crisis, a **new civilization** is emerging. It is an Earth-based civilization of sustainable human development. In this new civilization, people will increasingly embody a consciousness of being part of the living Earth, of being part of the life force of our beautiful planet. We are all Earthlings. All people and all life forms are our brothers and sisters. We have a common future or no future at all. In the new civilization, people will embody behavior that is empathic and compassionate. People will embody a culture of peace, creativity, and learning. People will embody systems, policies, and institutions of equality, justice, and universal participation in decision-making. And if we do not create such a civilization, the alternative will be chaos, tyranny, suffering, and systems collapse.

In this critical decade, we must build a new civilization of sustainable human development, country by country, organization by organization, and most importantly, community by community.

The author's first experiences in community development were on the West Side of Chicago in the 1960s, working with an NGO in the African American ghetto. The NGO, the Institute of Cultural Affairs (ICA), was catalyzing a demonstration of how any community in the world could transform itself economically, socially, culturally, and politically. The pilot project was named 5th City. As people from outside the community, the NGO's role was to empower, train, equip, and connect the residents to do their own development.

We worked within a geographically delimited area and involved all the people, all age groups, and addressed all issues simultaneously, which we called integrated human development. We found through hard experience that symbols were the keys to community renewal. 5th City created songs, stories, and symbols that inspired residents to transform their community. There was a sculpture of the Iron Human on 5th Avenue, songs of empowerment in the preschool and in community meetings, and stories of heroes doing the impossible and creating a new world. Residents understood that what they were doing was on behalf of the whole world. 5th City was understood as a global human development demonstration project, and this was perhaps the most powerful motivation of all.

And, we learned that every community has a depth contradiction that is blocking its development that must be addressed. For 5th City, it was the victim image – people felt that they were powerless to create their own destiny. One way to counter this was to create empowering songs for the preschool children such as this one: "I am always falling down. But I know what I can do. I can pick myself up and say to myself. I'm the greatest too. It doesn't matter if you're big or small. You live now if you live at all. I am always falling down. But I know what I can do."

Based on the 5th City model, we created a participatory planning methodology that any community could use. We took it around the world and launched human development projects in the 24 time zones of the planet. The author helped launch two projects in the Republic of Korea, one on Cheju Island in the village of Kwang Yung Il Ri and one near the DMZ, Kuh Du I Ri. He also worked in village projects in Jamaica (Woburn Lawn) and Venezuela (Cano Negro). Eventually our NGO was working in hundreds of communities around the world including mass replication in India and Kenya.

When the author joined UNDP in 1990, he helped design and launch a global program to renew urban slums and squatter settlements around the world. The LIFE program (the Local Initiative Facility for the Urban Environment) worked in 12 pilot countries around the world in 300 cities. Residents worked in collaboration with local authorities and NGOs in improving their living environment. We called this "local-local dialogue." Through small grants for micro projects local people improved their solid waste management, potable water, environmental health and education and drainage, gender equality, and created local jobs.

At the beginning of this century, the nations of the world launched through the UN the Millennium Development Goals (MDGs) initiative. This was the first time in history that the world had agreed on tangible, time bound goals to improve the lives of people all around the world. These goals included eradicating poverty, empowering women, providing early education, protecting the environment, and mitigating HIV/

AIDS and malaria. Many of us in the UN believed that the key to achieving these goals was in their localization. Therefore, we launched initiatives to localize the MDGs in local communities around the world, such as Decentralizing the MDGs through Innovative Leadership (DMIL).

And now, here we are together in the UN Public Service Awards Forum which itself is an important effort to create a new civilization, country by country, community by community, lesson by lesson, story by story. We are here in Dar to advance that noble cause.

III. 21st Century Public Service and Transformative Leadership for Sustainable Human Development

Public service in the 21st century faces many challenges and opportunities. Amid the breaking down of an old civilization and the emergence of a new civilization, public service is now called more than ever to provide innovative leadership for sustainable human development.

There are many styles of leadership which follow a developmental progression (Dennis Emberling). First, leadership can be authoritarian, exploitative, and coercive. Here the leader is the boss, dictator, or employer. Next leadership can be bureaucratic with the focus on rules and roles, Here the leader is a manager, administrator or "parent." The third stage of leadership is pragmatic with a focus on results. Here the leader is a guide. Next, leadership can be based on values and principles. Here the leader is a facilitator, coordinator, or coach. And finally, leadership can be systems-based with a concern for multiple perspectives. Here there are no managers but true delegation of responsibility to all members of the team.

What then are the most effective means in this critical decade with which to build a new civilization, country by country, community by community, organization by organization? **Transformative leadership** approaches are an essential key to unlock the potential of countries, communities, and organizations. From four decades of international development work, the author is aware of many leadership methods and approaches which have been applied within UN programs, national governments, NGOs, private companies, local communities, and universities. A few of the many effective ways of building creative countries, organizations, and communities through innovative leadership follow.

Change requires new systems, policies, and institutions but these alone are not enough. To create effective change, we must also transform individual consciousness and behavior and collective culture. These four dimensions of leadership based on Ken Wilber's quadrants of integral development are all essential: change that is both individual and collective, and internal and external.

Four Quadrant Integral Framework		
	Interior	**Exterior**
Individual	Consciousness Mindset Awareness Values Attitudes	Behavior Interpersonal Relational Partnerships Group Skills

Four Quadrant Integral Framework		
	Interior	**Exterior**
Collective	Culture Myths/Stories Rituals/Rites Symbols Norms	Environment Organizations Institutions Systems Policies

The individual/interior dimension of integral leadership includes the consciousness, mindset, awareness, values, and attitudes of the leader and his/her development of these in other individuals. The individual/exterior dimension includes the individual behavior of the leader, interpersonal relations, partnerships and group skills, and her/his development of these with other individuals. The collective/interior dimension of leadership includes the leader's work with and transformation of cultural beliefs and values, myths and stories, rituals and rites, symbols, and norms for the betterment of society. And, the collective/exterior dimension of leadership includes the leader's care and re-creation of the natural and built environment, organizations, institutions, systems, and policies.

Within each of these quadrants of leadership, we must work on four levels of transformation: physical/sensory, psychological/historic, mythic/symbolic, and unitive/spiritual. These four levels as delineated by Dr. Jean Houston in her social artistry work are all essential for effective change to take place.

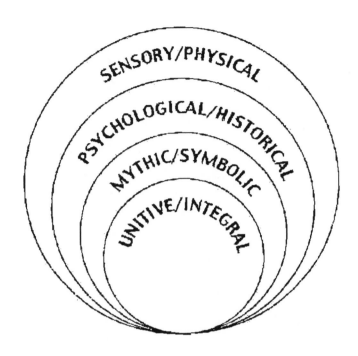

The sensory/physical level of social artistry leadership concerns the enhancement and activation of a leader's senses especially of deep listening and visionary seeing but also of touch, taste, and smell to be fully present to one's physical existence. This level includes the keen use of all the senses in relation to the natural and built environment, culture, and individual and group behavior. The psychological/historical level of social artistry leadership includes the deepening of individual and collective memory and emotion, personal psychological history, personal story, dream, and reflection, both in the leader and those the leader serves. The mythic/

symbolic level of social artistry leadership includes the use and powerful interpretation of myths, stories, heroes/heroines, and symbols of culture and religion to motivate the society to reach its human development goals. The unitive/integral level of social artistry leadership includes the experience and mysterious awareness of the unity and interconnectedness of all of life, a sense of oneness with others, self transcendence, spirituality, deep motivation, love, and a sense of calm and trust.

The third set of methods that is part of innovative leadership is the Technology of Participation or ToP. This array of effective leadership methods was developed by the Institute of Cultural Affairs (ICA) with which the author worked for 21 years. ToP includes, among others, methods of effective group discussion, group workshops and strategic planning.

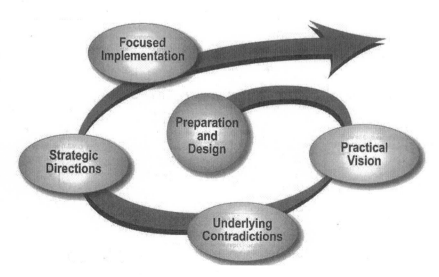

The ORID group conversation method takes people on a four part journey from Observation (what do you notice about the topic?), to Reflection (what are your associations and feelings about this?), to Interpretation (what does this mean for you?), and finally, to the Decisional (what relationship do you decide to take to this?) concerning what to do because of the discussion.

The ToP workshop method includes six steps: 1) deciding the rational and experiential objectives, 2) setting the context, 3) brainstorming, 4) grouping of data, 5) naming of clusters of data, and 6) reflecting on the group's consensus.

The ToP strategic planning process uses the workshop method for each step and enables a community or organization to 1) articulate the shared vision of their hoped-for future, 2) analyze what could block or enable that vision, 3) create broad strategic directions to achieve the vision, 4) identify tactical systems to achieve the strategies, and 5) decide what discrete actions or "implementaries" in what timeframe will do the job.

These are only three of many innovative leadership approaches that have been effectively applied around the world with governments, NGOs, local communities, and corporations. If made further use of in public service, public administration and governance over the coming years, they can have profound results both for the individual leader her/himself and for those with whom she/he works and serves as a leader. If a designated or elected leader makes use of these types of innovative methods, whole organizations, institutions, and communities will begin to mirror and emulate the leader's own awareness and prowess creating a powerful multiplying effect throughout the society. Can you imagine the use of any of these leadership approaches in a cabinet meeting, a parliament, or a city council, and what a difference they could make?

As we work together in this global forum, everyone is invited to make use of the most creative leadership methods and approaches that we know or can invent.

IV.   **The Global Forum Workshops and Follow up Actions**
This year, the overall theme of the United Nations and Africa Public Service Forum is: Transformative Leadership in Public Administration and Innovation in Governance: Creating a Better Life for All. In the two-day workshops of the Forum, the four thematic areas are:

1. Leading with integrity and inventiveness in public governance
2. Engaging citizens and civil society organizations to promote effectiveness, accountability and transparency in reconstruction and recovery strategies after natural disasters
3. African e-leadership capacity development
4. Leading innovations in gender-responsible service delivery

Each workshop includes panels and participatory discussion allowing each participant's insights and experience to inform the recommendations of the Forum.

With a social philosophy inspired by the Universal Declaration of Human Rights and considering the challenges and opportunities of this Critical Decade, the Forum workshops provide an unparalleled opportunity for the participants to articulate new pathways of transformative leadership and innovative governance. These pathways will in turn help clarify social discourse about future global, national, and local scenarios and inspire people around the world to do what is needed at this moment in history to bring into being a new civilization of sustainable human development.

The four workshops taken together will identify and delineate a new style and practice of leadership and governance that embodies integrity, creativity, participation of all the people in a society, gender equity, and use of information and communication technology and social networking. This is what is meant by transformative leadership - leadership that can respond effectively and profoundly to the multitude of challenges facing humanity at this critical moment and facilitate the creation of a new civilization.

Transformative leadership moves a society from a problem-solving mode to a whole systems design mode. It helps transform individual mindsets, values, and behavior, and collective culture and institutions. The transformative leader is deeply concerned and committed to creating the conditions in a society that enable each woman, man, and child to realize her/his full potential. Transformative leadership makes use of participatory, interactive methods to ensure that each person's voice and wisdom is heard and felt in social dialogue and policy making.

The transformative leader is a social artist and makes use of myths, stories, rituals, symbols, and metaphors to motivate the society to imagine and reach its future vision. Transformative leadership makes use of the very latest information technologies to enable the population to participate in governance processes at every level. The transformative leader is a person of deep personal integrity and empathy who manifests compassion for other people. He/she is committed to being the servant of the people in helping everyone to live well and to die well. Transformative leadership is responsive to present and potential danger and disasters and helps prepare and engage the population in doing what is needed to avert and deal with natural disasters such as climate chaos and human-made suffering such as armed conflict. The transformative leader has a profound belief in universal human rights and is a powerful advocate for the empowerment of women, minorities, elders, and youth.

Transformative leadership works to create strong democratic institutions and processes of governance. If transformative leadership were found in legislatures, executive offices, bureaucracies, courts, electoral commissions, NGOs, and corporations, what a transformation we would see in the larger society! The transformative leader does everything in her/his power to help make a better life for all the people. To do this, he/she manages her/his ego, pride, greed, fear, anger and hatred and practices concern for and understanding toward all people.

The four workshops are designed to be interactive and participatory so that each participant's experience, ideas, insights, and lessons can flow into the creation of new plans, programs and tools of transformative leadership and innovative governance. In each workshop there will be a few speakers or panels to spark thinking and dialogue. Next, there will be a series of participatory processes led by group facilitators who will ask question after question after question to solicit the ideas of each participant. These ideas will be put together in new ways to create fresh insights that together will inform new tools and programs of leadership and governance. Throughout the process the guiding vision will be to "build a better life for all.

Following the Forum, the participants will return to their countries, organizations and communities with renewed vision and practical tools for the betterment of their societies. They will stay networked electronically and will continue to challenge and encourage each other. They will make use of new methods of leadership and will help create new institutions of participatory governance. They will design new systems and structures, as well as new policies, programs, and projects that will put into practice the insights gained in the Forum.

Concluding Questions

What if these four days in Dar marked a turning point in human history - from despair to hope, from greed to compassion, from impoverishment to empowerment? What if We the Participants are indeed the people that the world has been waiting for? What if we are the catalysts and servants that history requires currently? What if we can mobilize people in such a way as to respond to climate chaos, increasing poverty, the HIV/AIDS pandemic, gender-inequality and economic collapse? What if we embody integrity, creativity, effectiveness, accountability, and transparency in everything we say and do?

What if we are the transformative leaders who call our fellow and sister citizens to join us in the greatest and noblest of tasks – to Build the Earth - to create a New Civilization - to catalyze Sustainable Human Development? What if these are indeed the times and we are indeed the people?

4

"Innovative Leadership to Engage Citizens in Self-Governance and Development"

UN Public Service Awards and Global Forum 2012

New York City
26 – 27 June 2012

One year later, I gave the fourth call to action, this time in New York City at the annual UN global forum. The theme of the forum was "Innovation and Citizen's Engagement for Effective Governance." I also facilitated a workshop during the forum. This is the first time I spoke about an emerging empathic civilization.

Introduction
The aim of this paper and talk is to explore the context and approaches for how to develop innovative institutional and

leadership capacities for citizen engagement in service delivery. First, a brief overview of our historical moment of crisis and opportunity is provided. Next, an emerging empathic civilization of sustainable human development is explored. Following, the critical role of citizen engagement in self-governance and development is outlined. Finally, how to develop innovative and integral leadership and institutional capacities is articulated.

I. **Time of Crisis and Transformation**

We live in what is likely the most turbulent and transformative time in human history. The very future of life on Earth is at stake. In my case, my four-year-old grandson, Phoenix, and my two-year-old granddaughter, Mariela, remind me again and again of my care and passion for a positive future of life on this planet. We face multiple crises any one of which could be definitive. However, for us humans a *whole system transition* is underway – this is a transformation in the interconnected web of social, economic, political, cultural, and environmental forces and factors.

Climate chaos due to an economy based on fossil fuels is changing our planetary ecology endangering life support systems. We see ample evidence that temperatures are rising, that coastal cities will be flooded, and islands will be submerged. Droughts, desertification, and massive storms will increase. Food production will collapse. We are amidst a massive die-back of species. Oceans are becoming sick. Water scarcity is a cause for international conflicts. Mass migrations will take place as people search for a livable environment.

Fiscal and economic systems are careening out of control with austerity policies causing great harm to countless people. Money has become divorced from the care of people and nature. Profit for a tiny few has become a higher value than justice or equality for the vast majority.

Democratic governance systems have been captured by corporations and wealthy individuals overwhelming the voices of most citizens. Oligarchy and the plutocracy of the military-industrial complex are fighting to maintain their control of our societies and resources.

Fundamentalisms of all sorts are at war with an empirical, scientific worldview and the principles of inclusiveness and respect for differences of opinion. The rights of women – 50% of humanity – are being violated and pushed back in alarming ways. Culture wars continue to erode human rights.

HIV/AIDS and other new and old diseases are rampant causing widespread suffering. Health care systems have become too costly or are non-existent. Public education is being threatened and denigrated.

This is a time to "do or die." Either we do what is necessary to survive, or we may die as a species along with many other species.

II. Emerging Empathic Civilization of Sustainable Human Development

What then is the big picture, the overarching narrative of our times? Is it inevitable that we are moving through a time of systems collapse, suffering, and death? Or could something else be emerging? What if the breaking down of our unsustainable, unjust, authoritarian, unequal, and divisive systems is forcing us to re-invent these systems based on healthy and hopeful principles of sustainability, justice, participation, equality, and inclusiveness? What if these crises are really opportunities to redesign our societies as part of a new empathic civilization of sustainable human development that works for everyone?

Our current systems are not working for the human population or for other life forms. Ours is a time of crisis that can wake us from this nightmare, so that we can create a new way of being, a way of well-being for and on this Earth. Empathy has always been a deep part of the human psyche and is now being called by necessity, for survival's sake, to emerge as the driving force for a new civilization of mutuality and care. Every day it is proven again and again that people care about each other including those who are far away and from different nations, cultures, religions, and races. Human beings are fundamentally empathic because we are deeply interconnected one with another and recognize ourselves in each other. We each want happiness and health. We feel each other's suffering and joy. We are a big family of brothers and sisters which includes other life forms as well. Seven billion human beings are present on this Earth today with their unique intelligence, creativity, compassion, and understanding to take us through this dangerous transition. This is the moment of citizens to the rescue.

The new civilization will be based on a social contract of the interdependence of people with each other and with natural systems. The renewable energy of sun, wind, and water will sustain our social and economic life. The protection of natural systems of soil, water, plants, and animals will be embodied both in collective law and individual behavior. Governance systems will be based on the needs and voice of all the people not just the economic, political, and cultural elites. Accountability, transparency, and responsiveness will be present at all levels of government.

Fiscal systems will be designed to provide equity to all people. Global and local economies will be concerned about the rights and well-being of workers and the environment. Health care and education will be universal rights in policy and practice. Cultural diversity will flourish, and people will delight in their differences and enjoy learning from each other's knowledge and wisdom. Consumption and production will be replaced as the highest good of society by mutual learning, care, artistic expression, and other forms of creativity.

This new civilization will be the flowering of the planetary and human project. Or, as Pierre Teilhard de Chardin put it, "the task before us now, if we would not perish, is to shake off our ancient prejudices and to build the Earth." Is this a vision of utopia? I would submit that we have a radical choice to make – either to move toward a sustainable and humanizing world or a world of endless dystopia of chaos and suffering.

III. Critical Role of Citizen Engagement and Innovation in Self-Governance and Development

Around the world citizens are rising with new energy for transformation. The Arab Spring and the Occupy Wall Street

movement are two manifestations of this. People are demanding that they participate and lead in their own governance
and development. It is time to move beyond the control of
corporatocracy, plutocracy, oligarchy, sexism, and militarism.
Citizens can govern their societies through their own intelligence, voice, and energy. Education, health care, justice, livelihood, shelter, food, water, and sanitation are universal human
rights and can be provided for all, to all and by all. Current
policies of austerity and scarcity are damaging and dangerous
and must be replaced by policies of sufficiency and sharing.

Citizens around the world have organized as nongovernmental organizations (NGOs,) community-based organizations (CBOs), women's groups and youth groups to engage in
self-governance and development. Civil society is now seen
clearly as one of the three governance actors, the other two
being government and the private sector. The environmental
movement and the human rights movement are the direct
voices of citizens to create a sustainable and human world.
To empower these citizen movements, new and effective
institutional and leadership capacities are needed.

We see around the world NGOs and CBOs collaborating
with local authorities and local businesses to improve the
living environment in low income settlements. We see NGOs
and CBOs improving sanitation systems and waste management, providing clean drinking water, and starting clinics and
community schools. We see NGOs and CBOs speaking out
for the rights of the poor, minorities, women, youth, and the
elderly. We see NGOs giving voice on behalf of other species, the oceans, air, and soil. People everywhere are waking

up to their interconnectedness through social media, mass media and travel and know their rights and their power to direct the course of history.

Knowledgeable, engaged citizens – of communities, nations, and the globe – are the key to confronting the over-whelming challenges facing us and creating a new empathic civilization of sustainable human development.

IV.   Developing Innovative Leadership and Institutional Capacities to Empower and Engage Citizens

No longer can leadership be by command-and-control. Absolute authority does not work and is inappropriate for a race of intelligent, creative beings. Local and national govern-ments are being called to a new style of leadership to empower and engage citizens in their own governance and develop-ment. The type of leadership needed at this time of crisis and opportunity must be integral, facilitative, and creative.

Traditionally, change processes have focused exclusively on institutional arrangements, policies, and systems. This collective-exterior leadership is critical but is not sufficient. Change must also happen within the culture itself – the col-lective interior – by changing collective values and norms through motivating, transformative stories, rites, and symbols. Change must happen in individual values and behavior – the individual interior and individual exterior dimensions – changing mindsets and perspectives as well as relational and interpersonal behavior. This is integral leadership – working to change collective institutions and culture and individual mindsets and behavior. In addition to having the right legal frameworks in place, we must have the right individual and collective values and behaviors moving our societies toward a more sustainable and human future.

The facilitative leader sees her/himself as a guide who enables groups of people to think, analyze, plan and act together through participatory, interactive processes. The facilitative leader asks questions of people that allow them to journey together in a structured manner toward productive outcomes. Facilitation of citizen participation is essential to motivate and call forth the creativity and energy of all the people to respond to the massive challenges facing us today. Facilitation can be learned as a new type of leadership that does not control outcomes but provides participatory processes that allow citizens to create the policies and services that are most important to them.

Facilitation requires skill and patience, an ability to listen deeply and a willingness to allow citizens to chart pathways of good governance and effective development. The facilitative leader has the skill to lead productive discussions, analytical and problem-solving workshops, strategic planning exercises and whole system design processes. The facilitative leader asks people to articulate their hoped for vision of the future, the factors that could enable or inhibit reaching that vision, the strategic directions that would carry them toward their vision taking into account the inhibiting and enhancing factors, and the implementation-action plan and timeline that they will commit to in the day to day.

Government must provide a multitude of opportunities of facilitated citizen dialogue and decision making through forums, workshops, conferences, online chat rooms, web-sites, and social media.

The creative leader is a social artist who awakens and enlivens peoples' capacities in the dimensions of the sensory/physical, psychological/ historical, mythic/symbolic, and unitive/spiritual. The creative leader provides processes by which people can access their own creativity, intuition, motivation, courage, vision, and genius in solving problems and designing new systems. The leader as social artist enables citizens to deepen their capacities of body, mind, and spirit to release their full potential as human beings. The creative leader makes use of individual and group processes, both face to face and online, that stimulate the best thinking, doing, and being in others that is possible.

The integral, facilitative, and creative leader helps turn challenges into opportunities for sustainable human development. Government officials who learn and practice these skills find themselves becoming true civil servants – the servants of the people – that they have pledged to be as elected or appointed leaders.

Conclusion

Over this day and one half, we will practice integral, facilitative, and creative leadership as we share our knowledge with each other and make recommendations for ourselves, member states, and the United Nations. We will listen deeply for insights in the presentations and discuss interactively at our tables using a series of questions. As Rilke says, we will be "living the questions." We will be the People of the Question.

We will be asking "what if" and acting "as if" it is possible. We will become an emerging Community of Practice on governance and development.

Related to the concept of Gross National Happiness, happiness will not be our goal but our way of being as we catalyze well-being for ourselves and all others. A sense of hope will carry us through this tumultuous time of crisis and danger and the lure of a possible-future will draw us toward it — a new empathic civilization of sustainable human development. Innovative leaders within government and throughout our societies are needed to help humanity through this great transition. If not us, who? If not now, when?

5

"Wake Up Time On Planet Earth!"

Keynote for the ICAI 8th Global Conference on Human Development

Kathmandu, Nepal
30 October 2012

*F*our months later, I traveled to Kathmandu to give the fifth critical decade call to action. This keynote was for an ICA International global conference on human development.

From Serving People & Planet: *"It was meaningful being back in Nepal for my sixth visit since 1969. Dr. Tatwa Timsina had invited me to make the keynote. He circulated at the conference a book,* Changing Lives, Changing Societies, *that had recently been published by ICA Nepal. I was happy to have written two of the chapters in the book, one co-authored with Tatwa. Again, I visited and circumambulated my special*

Buddhist temple in Kathmandu, Swayambhunath Stupa." (page 188)

(Nepali music is playing/Earth banner is above and behind.)

Namaste! (palms together)

Please relax your body and focus your mind on your breath, just sitting, just being, just enjoying this moment. (3 min.)

"I teach only suffering and the relief of suffering." The man who said these words 2,500 years ago was born not far from here in Lumbini, Nepal. His name, Siddhartha Gautama of the Shakya clan. We know him as the Buddha, the one who woke up – the awakened one.

Suffering – 2.5 billion people live on less than $2 per day. 2.6 billion lack access to sanitation. 1 billion have no access to safe water. 10 million preventable child deaths occur each year. How do we relieve suffering?

I am grateful to the great people and land of Nepal, the birthplace of Lord Buddha, the roof top of the world, for welcoming and hosting us in this global human development conference. Thanks especially to Tatwa Timsina for your vision and commitment to make this event a reality and for asking me to speak to you. Thanks to Larry Philbrook for your consistent, energizing leadership of ICAI. Thanks to the conference organizers, sponsors, theme leaders, sherpas and facilitators for your creative, hard work – especially Kushendra Mahat, Ishu Subba, Juju, Nimesh and many others.

Please turn to someone near you and share your name and what you hope to accomplish here this week.

The person standing here has a simple resume: ICA – 21 years; UNDP – 16 years; New York University – 5 years; from local community projects to global policy advice and now teaching and consulting.

This is my sixth time to be in mysterious Nepal, the first being 43 years ago when I traveled around the world with a few ICA colleagues and fell deeply in love with planet Earth, her mountains, oceans and living beings. In Nepal, I have witnessed a live goat sacrifice, meditated in ancient temples, flown by Mt. Everest, travelled to the Eastern region, met with villagers on a hilltop, launched a UNDP project on Decentralized Approaches to HIV/AIDS Mitigation with Tatwa Timsina and Jan Sanders and, as a Fulbright specialist, designed a Masters curriculum on training and development with Tatwa, Kushendra and others. Nepal and I have changed some since then. I now have two beautiful grandchildren.

This is my third time to address a global ICAI conference, first in Oaxtapec, Mexico, in 1988, the year we dissolved the collective structures of ICA's core group of families; then in 1994 in Lonavala, India, during a plague. I wonder what will happen now and next?

And you are here! Let us see the hands of the women. The men. The young ones. Who is the youngest? The elders. Who is oldest? Who is from an NGO? Government? Business? Academia? Media? Intergovernmental? Others? Who is here from . . .? (mention each country, one by one, and ask people to raise their hands.) Who is with ICA? Other than ICA? Who came the longest journey here?

There are also virtual participants around the world who are online. Who are some of them? From where?

Our space is here, and now is our time. These are indeed the times!

Do you like poetry? I would like to read you a poem by the incomparable Nepali poet Laxmi Prasad Devkota:

Look at the strumpet-tongues advancing of shameless leadership!

At the breaking of the backbones of the people's rights!

When the sparrow-headed bold prints of black lies on the papers,

Challenge the hero in me called Reason,

With conspiracy false,

Then redden hot my cheeks, my friend,

And their color is up.

when the unsophisticated folk quaff off black poison with their ears

Taking it for ambrosia,

And that before my eyes, my friend,

Then every hair rises on end,

Like the serpent-tresses of the Gorgons,

Every one so irritated!

When I see the tiger pouncing upon the innocent deer,

Or the big fish after the smaller ones,

Then even into my corroded bones, my friend,

The terrible strength of the soul of Dadhichi--the sage,

Enters and seeks utterance.

Like a clouded day crashing down to earth in the thunderbolt,

When man regards a man as no man,
Then gnash my teeth and grind my jaws, set with the two
and thirty teeth,
Like Bhimsen's teeth, the terror-striking hero's,
And then,
Rolling round my fury-reddened eyeballs,
With an inscrutable sweep,
I look at this inhuman human world
Like a tongue of fire.
(From "The Lunatic")

What has brought us to this moment? Scientists tell us that around 14 billion years ago there was a great flaring forth of time, space, and energy, coalescing in atoms and light, evolving into galaxies and stars, then into planets and finally into plants and animals. And here we are today on our gorgeous planet Earth. What will be going on in another 14 billion years?

Historians tell us that there are around 5,000 years of recorded history. What do you hope will going on in another 5,000 years?

The industrial age began 250 years ago. What could be happening in another 250 years?

Well, for me, we are living in the most critical decade and century in human history – a moment of crisis and opportunity. Why do I believe that?

Everything is changing, everything. This is a time of whole systems transformation and "raplexity" – rapidity plus complexity. We are in mortal danger, and therefore, we have the possibility to reinvent the human enterprise.

Because of the last 200 years of burning fossil fuels, massive amounts of carbon have been released into the atmosphere, now over 350 parts per million, and planet Earth is heating up. Glaciers and ice caps are melting, including here in the Himalayas. Sea levels are rising. Coastal cities and islands will be submerged. (Nepal is lucky to "land locked"!) Oceans are becoming acidic; and there is a massive die back of species both marine and terrestrial. Mega storms are increasing. Droughts and wildfires are spreading. Water and food shortages are accelerating. These phenomena are not theoretical but observable. They are happening now. Our planet has already changed and if we humans do not alter our individual and collective behavior, our planet will soon become inhospitable to life.

But we can change. We must stop the fossil fuel industries of oil, gas, and coal (death-energy) and rapidly promote renewable energy from sun, water, wind, geo-thermal and algae (life-energy.) This is the green energy revolution. Nepal is fortunate to have an abundance of hydropower potential. There is a global environmental movement at work including 350, Green Peace and many others. It is time to embrace life or to face extinction.

Because of the last 5,000 years of male dominance (the patriarchy) women's wisdom has not played its necessary role in the design and management of our societies. Women have been kept silent, subservient, abused, trapped at home and pregnant. They have not been allowed to exercise their human rights of speech, choice, career, and leadership. This has resulted in overly masculinized societies that promote and celebrate violence, harmful competition, technology without heart, and warfare.

Improvements for women have taken place, yet we have a long way to go. And in some parts of the world there is a backlash against women's rights. That is why 14-year-old Malala Youstafzai was shot recently in Pakistan by the Taliban, and why the Republicans in my country want to ban abortion. As the patriarchy dies out, some men are fighting back to control women's bodies and minds. But this must not stand. Our societies need the participation and leadership of women at every level of society and in full partnership with men. Our societies need feminine perspectives, wisdom and actions of nurture, relationship, and compassion. Without gender equality and the empowerment of women we will not make it as a species.

Our modern economies are based on capital, profit, debt and interest and the global gambling casino of investing. Money accumulation for a few has become more important than the wellbeing of all people and nature. Economic enterprises, based on fossil fuel energy, pollute the air, water, and soil, and abuse human labor. Our economies are killing us, other life forms, and our planetary ecosystems. Fiscal policy is made by global elites that control the formation and movement of capital through central banks and investment firms. The 1% has become consumed by greed and power. Austerity for the masses and opulence for the few is not the human way.

But we are waking up! Sacred economics (Charles Eisenstein) shows us that capital should not be based on debt and interest. Bartering is increasing. Local currencies are being developed. There is a global movement, including Transition Towns (Rob Hopkins), which promotes growing home gardens, buying local, using less gasoline, and traveling less and buying from companies which respect nature and workers. We can and must create local, national, and global economies that are pro-people and pro-planet. We must shift from an economy based on greed to an economy of generosity.

The democratic experiment of the past 200 years is faltering badly around the world. Oligarchy, plutocracy and corporatocracy are masquerading as democratic regimes. The elites are manipulating democratic institutions to maintain control of political, economic, and military power. We are experiencing a deep crisis of governance. As Nepal knows, it is not easy to move from a monarchy to a constitutional democracy. It takes changes in mindset, behavior, and culture as well as the formation of democratic institutions. And as Nepal knows well, a lasting peace involves profound changes in the human psyche as well as in social organization.

Local people around the world are rising as we see in the Arab Spring, the Occupy (Wall Street) Movement, and the anti-austerity movement in Europe. People are voting with their bodies in the street. Local people are demanding a say in their own governance. Participatory self-governance can be our future if we do not give up. We can create meta-modern democracies, as Hordur Torfarson of Iceland names them.

We humans are still plagued by illiteracy, illness, ignorance, and prejudice. Our educational systems are not adequate for all the people. Likewise, our health systems are tragically unable to provide even basic care to all people everywhere and people suffer senseless illnesses. Cultural and religious bigotry, fear and hatred are causing great harm to many. In our hearts, however, we know that everyone deserves a quality education and good healthcare. These are part of our universal human rights. We also need social safety nets to ensure care especially for the elderly and the poor. We can do this. We have the capacity. We have the resources. We must mobilize the political will to do so. We can live in mutual respect with people of different ethnic, religious and lifestyle choices realizing that in diversity is richness, beauty, and mutual learning.

As we investigate the future, two paths present themselves, either continued crisis and collapse or an emerging empathic civilization. We are here this week to share and search for strategies and initiatives that will take humanity toward sustainable human development. We know that we can build a world that works for everyone. We can create societies that enable each person to realize her/his full potential. We can create the possible human and the possible society. (Jean Houston) We can build the Earth. (Teilhard de Chardin)

We the people will prevail, and we are the people. The seven billion of us have the collective intelligence and will, not only to survive but to flourish. I stand in awe and gratitude for being alive at this critical moment in history and am committed to act on behalf of all. We are part of Those Who Care, the sensitive and response ones, who are waking up and are engaged in risk taking, innovation, reinvention, embodying, catalyzing, and creating the environments for human emergence.

The 350 movement is awakening people to climate chaos mitigation; Transition Towns is demonstrating a new lifestyle and economy; the Occupy movement is showing that non-violent resistance is necessary; and the Arab Spring is demanding political voice for the masses. Local people are on the rise. Women, who hold up half the sky, are stepping forward. Youth are leading the way as the emerging generation. NGOs and CBOs are showing that civil society is one of the three governance actors alongside government and business. People realize that we need energized government at every level – local, national, global – to promote the wellbeing of people and nature. Enlightened businesses are demonstrating corporate responsibility. Academia is calling for open, free education. Social media is enabling billions of local people to share their hopes and dreams as a global village.

Repeat after me (thrice): The task before us now/if we would not perish/is to shake off our ancient prejudices/and to build the Earth! (Pierre Teilhard de Chardin)

I can't think of six more important areas to work on this week than developing innovative leadership, inventing open education, developing local communities, creating a viable planet, promoting peace and good governance, and developing the human, financial and technical resources needed for all of this.

This is one integrated dialogue and task this week, is it not? A viable planet is the global context. Water, air, soil, plants, and animals are our brothers and sisters. Community development is the local, and everyone is local. A new sense of leadership is at the heart of each theme and leads the way through integral frameworks (Ken Wilber), Social Artistry (Jean Houston) and the Technology of Participation (ICA), among others. Open education creates the cultural mindsets and skills needed. (Tatwa's new master's degree program in training and development provides a model curriculum.) Peace and good governance are the political systems that will make everything work together to support all living beings. And, access to abundant resources is part of a new economy of generosity, empathy, and compassion.

Each theme group needs to identify strategies and initiatives that promote their theme in relation to the five other themes that: 1) change individual mindsets and values; 2) change individual behaviors; 3) change collective cultural beliefs and values; and 4) change collective policies, institutions and systems. (Ken Wilbur)

In the midst of an incredible array of crises, I believe that it is possible to save all sentient beings and all life on Earth, to build an Empathic Civilization (Jeremy Rifkin), to create a world that works for everyone and to reinvent societies that enable each human being to realize her/his full potential.

To do this we will need to care for ourselves. We need to engage daily in spiritual practices such as meditation, yoga, and journaling. We need to be willing to change, change, and change some more. We need to break a habit each day. We must be true to our deepest values and vows. We must *be the change* that is needed in the world (Gandhi.) Happiness is not our goal but our path. We can wake up every moment to peace, happiness, compassion and understanding.

This group is gathered for a very precious moment. We are the ones we have been waiting for. This is our chance for breakthrough thinking, doing and being, for innovation, creativity, boldness, and risk taking.

To the theme groups, stand and be sent forward: viable planet, local community, leadership, education, peace and good governance, and resources.

To Nepal, believe in yourself, your genius, your destiny. To all other countries, be your greatness. To the women, know that the rise of women and of the feminine in each of us will heal us all. To the youth, you are the future emergent. To the men: change, change, change. To the ICA, do not rest on your laurels, keep learning. To all other organizations, be your unique gift to the world.

When we leave here, we will be a virtual Community of Practice – sharing questions and knowledge, encouraging, modeling, risking, challenging, collaborating, supporting, and communicating. We will be a movement and a social media blizzard. During the rest of this decade, this is it, pull out all the stops.

For the rest of this century, let us shock the world with human development! Let us delight the planet with human emergence! I call us to step beyond that which is no longer and to move toward the not yet, to be the people of the wedge.

In the words of the English poet D.H. Lawrence written in 1916:

Not I, not I, but the wind that blows through me!/ A fine wind is blowing the new direction of Time [wind energy?]./ If only I let it bear me, carry me, if only it carry me!/ If only I am sensitive, subtle, oh, delicate, a winged gift!/ If only, most lovely of all I yield myself and am borrowed/ By the fine, fine wind that takes its course through the chaos of the world/ Like a fine, an exquisite chisel, a wedge-blade inserted;/ If only I am keen and hard like the sheer tip of a wedge/ Driven by invisible blows,/ The rock will split, we shall come at the wonder, we shall find the Hesperides [the Himalayas, Lumbini, our true home, our deepest heart]./ Oh, for the wonder that bubbles into my soul,/ I would be a good fountain, a good well-head,/ Would blur no whisper, spoil no expression./ What is the knocking?/ What is the knocking at the door in the night?/ It is somebody wants to do us harm./ No, no, it is the three strange angels [the 200 strange angels.]/ Admit them, admit them. ("Song of a Man Who Has Come Through")

It is wakeup time on planet Earth! Now is the Time! We are the People!

(Nepali Music Playing: Nepali Dancing!)

6

"Promoting Participatory Governance for Environmental Sustainability, Gender Equality, and Socio-Economic Justice"

UN Public Service Awards and Global Forum 2013

Manama, Bahrain
24 June 2013

*T*he sixth critical decade call to action was given in Bahrain to six hundred participants from around the world, eight months after the conference in Nepal. This was for the annual UN global forum with the theme of "Transformative e-Governance and Innovation: Creating a Better Future for All".

From Serving People & Planet*: "In June that year, I traveled for the first time to Manama, the capital of Bahrain, a
desert island nation between Saudi Arabia and Qatar. There I
made a plenary presentation on participatory governance to
600 government and NGO officials from around the world in
the UN Global Forum on Public Service (the presentation is on
the UNDESA website). After that, I helped design and participate in the forum's UN Expert Group Meeting on e-government.
One of the unusual events during the workshop was a dinner
hosted by the king at his palace in Manama. A treat after the
meeting was getting to drive a go-cart on the big track dressed
in racing suit and helmet. I was proud of myself even though I
didn't win. I survived, and that was sufficient." (page 189)*

May you and I and all beings realize peace, happiness,
wisdom, and compassion.

We are living in the most critical time in human history – a
moment of crisis and opportunity. Why do I believe that?

Everything is changing and everything is at risk. This is
a time of whole systems transformation. Life on Earth is in
mortal danger; and therefore, we have the necessity and the
possibility to reinvent the entire human enterprise to create
a better future for all.

Because of the last 200 years of burning fossil fuels, massive amounts of carbon have been released into the atmosphere, now at 400 parts per million exceeding the safe
limit of 350 parts per million. Planet Earth is heating up and
glaciers and ice caps are melting. Sea levels are rising, and
coastal cities and islands will be submerged. Oceans are
becoming acidic; and there is a massive die back of species

both marine and terrestrial. Mega storms are increasing, and droughts and wildfires are spreading. Water and food shortages will accelerate. These phenomena are not theoretical but observable. They are happening now. Our planet has already changed and if we humans do not alter our individual and collective behavior, our planet will soon become inhospitable to life and suffering will increase.

But we know what to do and are beginning to do it. We must stop burning oil, gas, and coal – death-energy – and rapidly promote renewable energy from sun, water, wind, geo-thermal and algae – life-energy. This is the green energy revolution. There is a global environmental movement at work including the UN, 350.org, Green Peace and many others. It is time to protect life itself or face massive die back. E-government can alert citizens to these trends and dangers and provide help and incentives for renewable energy use and for adaptation to crisis situations.

Because of the last 5,000 years of male dominance – the patriarchy – women's wisdom has not played its necessary role in the design and management of our societies. Women have often been kept silent, subservient, abused, trapped at home, and pregnant. They have not been allowed to exercise their human rights of speech, choice, career, and leadership. This has resulted in overly masculinized societies that promote and celebrate violence, harmful competition, technology without heart, and warfare.

We are waking up, and improvements for women are taking place, yet we have a long way to go. And in some parts of the world, there is a backlash against women's rights. That is why fourteen-year-old Malala Yousafzai was shot recently in Pakistan by the Taliban and why some Republicans in my country want to ban abortion. As patriarchy dies out, some men are fighting back to control women's bodies and minds. But this must not stand. Our societies need the participation and leadership of women at every level of society and in full partnership with men. Our societies need feminine perspectives, wisdom and actions of nurture, relationship, and compassion. Without gender equality and the empowerment of women we will not make it as a species. E-government can provide channels for women's voices to influence policy making as well as access to vital services to empower women's participation and leadership.

We humans are still plagued by illiteracy, illness, ignorance, and prejudice. Our educational systems are not adequate for all the people. Likewise, our health systems are tragically unable to provide even basic care to all people everywhere and people suffer senseless illnesses. Cultural and religious bigotry, fear and hatred cause great harm to many.

Yet in our hearts, we know that everyone deserves a quality education and good healthcare. These are universal human rights. We also need social safety nets to ensure care for the elderly and the poor. We can do this. We have the capacity and the resources. We must mobilize the political will to do so. We can live in mutual respect with people of different ethnic, religious and lifestyle choices realizing that in diversity are richness, beauty, and mutual learning. E-government can bring access to education and health closer to citizens especially the most vulnerable.

Our modern economies are based on capital, profit, debt, interest, and the global gambling casino of investing. Money accumulation for a few has become more important than the wellbeing of all people and nature. Economic enterprises, based on fossil fuel energy, pollute the air, water and soil, and abuse human labor. Our economies are killing us, other life forms, and our planetary ecosystems. Fiscal policy is made by global elites that control the formation and movement of capital through central banks and investment firms. The 1% has become comfortable with greed and power. Austerity for the masses and opulence for the few is not the human way.

But things are changing. Sacred economics as expounded by Charles Eisenstein shows us that capital should not be based on debt and interest. Bartering is increasing. Local currencies are being developed. There is a global movement, including Transition Towns founded by Rob Hopkins, which promotes growing home gardens, buying local, using less gasoline, traveling less, and buying from companies which respect nature and workers. We can and must create local, national, and global economies that are pro-people and pro-planet. We must shift from an economy based on greed to an economy of generosity. E-government can provide citizen access to necessary skills training, credit, and markets.

Every system of governance is in crisis. Autocracy is still with us, and the democratic experiment of the past 200 years is faltering badly around the world. Oligarchy, plutocracy, and corporatocracy are masquerading as democratic regimes. The elites are buying and manipulating democratic institutions (media, courts, legislatures, executives, voting) to maintain control of political, economic, and military power. Changes in mindset, behavior, and culture are needed as well as the formation of democratic institutions. A lasting peace involves profound changes in the human psyche as well as in social organization.

But local people around the world are rising as we see in the Occupy (Wall Street) Movement, the Arab Spring, the anti-austerity movement in Europe and the current demonstrations in Brazil and Turkey. People are voting with their bodies in the street. Local people are demanding a say in their own governance. E-government can bring policy making and service delivery closer to the people. Participatory self-governance can be our future if we do not give up. We can create meta-modern democracies as Hordur Torfarson describes from the experience of Iceland.

As we investigate the future, two paths present themselves, either continued crisis and collapse or an emerging empathic civilization. We humans are hardwired for empathy, compassion, and altruism. We must continue to evolve and manifest these qualities.

We are here this week to share and search for strategies and initiatives that will take humanity toward sustainable human development and a better life for all people. We know that we can build a world that works for everyone. We can create societies that enable each person to realize her/his full potential. We can create the possible human and the possible society as Jean Houston has said.

We the people will prevail, and we are the people. The seven billion of us have the collective intelligence and will, not only to survive but to flourish. I stand in awe and gratitude for being alive at this critical moment in history and am committed to act on behalf of all. You and I are part of Those Who Care, the sensitive and response ones, who are waking up and engaged in risk taking, innovation, reinvention, embodying, catalyzing, and creating the environments for human emergence.

The 350.org movement is awakening people to climate chaos mitigation; Transition Towns is demonstrating a new sustainable lifestyle and economy; the Occupy movement is showing that non-violent resistance is necessary; and the Arab Spring is demanding political voice for the masses. Local people are on the rise. Women, who hold up half the sky, are stepping forward. Youth are leading the way as the emerging generation. NGOs and CBOs are showing that civil society is one of the three governance actors alongside government and business. People realize that we need energized government at every level – local, national, global – to promote the wellbeing of people and nature. Enlightened businesses are demonstrating corporate responsibility. Academia is calling for open, free education. Social media is enabling billions of local people to share their hopes and dreams as a global village.

Let us say together the hopeful words of Pierre Teilhard de Chardin: Please repeat after me: The task before us now/ if we would not perish/is to shake off our ancient prejudices/ and to build the Earth!

E-government can make access to services closer to citizens and bring citizen choices and wisdom into the policy making process. E-government is one aspect of participatory governance and as such has an important role to play in promoting environmental sustainability, gender equality and socio-economic justice. E-government should make citizens aware of the crisis we face in our eco-systems of air, water, soil, plants, and animals, and what needs to be done by all citizens to protect the environment and ensure a sustainable ecosystem for millions of years to come. E-government must deal both with mitigation and adaptation to climate chaos. E-government should also promote gender equality by giving voice to women in policy making and leadership at every level of society. E-government should promote socio-economic justice by making services of education, health, skills training, credit, and marketing accessible to all citizens.

To close the digital divide, governments should ensure that every citizen has access to computers, smart phones, literacy, and electricity to participate in e-governance. Governments must also ensure that the views of citizens through e-government channels are taken with the greatest of seriousness in policy making and service delivery. Governments must be held accountable for corruption and must act in a transparent manner. Anything less than this would make e-government and e-governance technical glitter and a sham.

In this global forum, we will be discussing how to promote collaborative e-governance through innovation and Information/ Communication Technologies (ICTs), the transformative power of e-government for the post-2015 development agenda, the transfer of innovations for improved public service delivery in least developed countries, fostering participation in the context of the post-2015 development agenda, transforming public service delivery to advance gender equality, creating an enabling environment for entrepreneurship and economic development through innovation and e-government, leadership for transformational government, initiatives towards e-governance and sustainable public services, and essential leadership capacities and actions for transformational government.

I would remind us that in all our discussions our ultimate objective is to create a better world for all people and all life forms everywhere. This is a noble task. Let us give it our best creativity and full energy.

Thank you for your attention, commitment, and action.

May you and I and all beings realize peace, happiness, wisdom, and compassion.

7

"The Four Faces of War and Peace: Mindsets, Behaviors, Cultures, Systems"

Oklahoma City University Symposium on Creative Peace Building

Oklahoma City, Oklahoma, USA
7 March 2014

*E*ight months later, I gave the seventh critical decade call to action in Oklahoma City, USA This was six months after I launched my blog "A Compassionate Civilization".

From Serving People & Planet: "In March, at Oklahoma City University (OCU) I made a keynote presentation at the invitation of Rev. Dr. Mark Davies, OCU dean of arts and sciences, in a symposium on creative peacemaking. My topic was the "Four Faces of War and Peace." I based the talk on Ken

Wilber's quadrants of mindsets, behaviors, cultures, and sys-
tems. The participants actively dialogued with each other and
seemed to appreciate the presentation. (Video is on the inter-
net.) It was great being back on the Oklahoma prairie once
again. My brother, Duncan, had flown out from Asheville with
me, and his son Matthew, from Fairfield, Iowa, met us there
for the event. Other ICA colleagues [among the participants]
from Oklahoma and north Texas were present." (page 193)

OPENING
May all people everywhere, including you and me, realize
peace, happiness, understanding, and compassion.

A Cherokee prayer . . . "O' Great Spirit, help me always to
speak the truth quietly, to listen with an open mind when others
speak, and to remember the peace that may be found in silence."

We are so busy, rushing about here and there. Let us
begin this morning by relaxing our body and bringing our
mind to stillness and quiet. Please relax your body. Become
aware of your body, breath, and mind. (5 minutes) What did
you notice, experience?

Thank you, Mark Davies, and Terry Bergdall, for inviting me to this symposium and to Joe Meinhart for making
me feel welcome. It is very meaningful for me to be back in
my home state. I am happy and honored that my brother,
nephew, and many colleagues are present here this morning.

INTRODUCTIONS
Please turn to someone next to you and introduce yourself.
Share with them what your hopes are for this symposium

and its follow up. (5 minutes) Okay, now let us hear a few of the hopes expressed by the person who was speaking to you.

Who is from the farthest? Closest? Oldest? Youngest? Our gender balance? We are exactly the group needed to be this symposium and to conduct creative peacemaking in our lives and work.

I was born in Houston and grew up and went to university here in Oklahoma at OSU. My great grandparents, grandparents, and parents were Oklahomans. I am proud that our state logo has two symbols of peace covering an Osage shield: the calumet, or peace pipe, representing Native Americans, and the olive branch representing European Americans.

Since leaving Oklahoma, and after graduate school in Chicago, for the past 45 years I have worked in international development in 55 countries with the Institute of Cultural Affairs, the United Nations Development Programme, and now with New York University, the UN, and the East-West Center. I am married to an amazing Zen Buddhist priest and have two wonderful sons and two adorable grandchildren.

As you know, the UN is dedicated to peace and development. It is said that there can be no peace without development, and no development without peace. I have spent my life working on the development side, so that we may have a lasting peace. Thus, I am a development expert not a peace expert.

CONTEXT

Introduction:
I believe that we are living in the most critical time in human history. This is it. Everything is at stake. It is a time of whole systems transformation. A time of crisis and opportunity. We must move toward a compassionate civilization or settle for a dystopia of environmental and social chaos. Why do we need to be aware of this in a symposium about creative peacemaking? This is the socio-environmental context in which we must wage peace.

Climate Chaos
Extracting and burning fossil fuels is damaging our planet's ecosystems resulting in violence and harm to humans and other life forms. Sea rise from melting ice is submerging islands and coastlines. Mega storms are battering human settlements. Droughts and flooding are harming people and food production. Acidification is killing sea life. These are literally acts of war against our planet and life on Earth. Peacemaking is critically necessary. Promoting sustainable development is the peacemaking required. How do we do this? What is required of us?

Gender Inequality
Half of the human population is relegated to second class status and suffers violence and abuse from men. This is a war on women. Peacemaking is required. Promoting gender equality and ensuring the full partnership of women at all

levels of society is the peacemaking needed. How must we go about this? What is required of us?

Socio-economic Injustice

Social and economic injustice is doing violence and harm to billions of people as the rich control more and more resources and wealth. This is a war on the poor and the middleclass and peacemaking is greatly needed now. Socio-economic justice is the peacemaking required. What is needed to make this happen? What can we do about this?

Dysfunctional Governance

Plutocracy, corporatocracy, oligarchy, and authoritarian rule are doing violence and harm to billions of people around the world. These are acts of war against people's freedom, self-determination, and voice. Radical peacemaking is needed. Participatory governance is the peacemaking required. What action will turn the tide? What can we do here and now?

Cultural Intolerance

Intolerance of differences of race, culture, religion, ethnicity, class, age, sex, and sexual and gender orientation is doing violence and harm to billions of people around the world. This is open warfare against those who are different, weak or minorities. Peacemaking is sorely needed. Tolerance, understanding and opportunity for all are the acts of peacemaking needed. How do we ensure that this happens?

Conclusion:
We live in a world at war. Peacemaking is the life and death vocation of our time. How are you and I personally called to use our creativity and energy?

Who is most concerned about climate chaos? Gender inequality? Socio-economic injustice? Dysfunctional governance? Cultural intolerance?

I would like to read you a poem entitled "Peace" by Clifford Browder, which he wrote because of something Jean Houston said.

Peace is not
Sterile gauze, a snowflake, an insipid dove
It's feisty and rich
Don't let the war boys hog it all
The spit, the spice and the glamour.
Peace is potency
Reaching and sprouting
Budding and branching
It's lifting things
A good scrap
A hot wrestle and a cool scrub
Cleansing and hope.
Peace is the empowerment of dust
Whispers of the song before origin
As out of seed
The cathedral of the body builds itself
It's spasms and metamorphoses
The vertigo

of mind and dancing
With the fecundator
To the music of need.
Peace
It is little orange bees
Spotted ladybugs on white campions.
Late June with a stink of linden
Prickles and burrs
It's wild grapes in a bramble
A tough nut
Lovers churning
Through the night, at noon, in the morning
A juicy comeuppance
For the grim suppressors.
Peace
Is for the star-biters and the rooted.
Don't be dainty
Go at it
Hammer and tong.
Peace is not purity
Limp, neat and dry.
It's sexy.

FOUR FACES OF WAR AND PEACE: MIND, BEHAVIOR, CULTURE AND SYSTEMS

Introduction:
War involves acts of violence and harm, whereas peace includes dialogue and justice. Ken Wilber provides us with an

integral map which can help us see the four faces of war and peace. There are four dimensions to the map: Interior, Exterior; and Individual, Collective. At the intersections are: Mind (Individual/Interior), Behavior (Individual/Exterior), Culture (Collective/Interior), and Systems (Collective/Exterior).

Take a few minutes and write your thoughts on your handout in the quadrants, in each quadrant, the left column is for what you think is contributing to violence and harm or war in that particular dimension and the right column is what can promote dialogue and justice or peace. (five minutes) Share with the person next to you. (five minutes) Let us hear one example from each quadrant, both warmongering and peacemaking.

I would like to share a few of my thoughts about these four faces of war and peace for your consideration.

Mind (Individual/Interior)

Mind of Warmongering:
A violent, harmful mind emerges as negative emotions arise from our confusion about our true nature of compassion and wisdom. When we separate our self from others, negative emotions of fear, anger, hatred, greed, and pride take root. These negative emotions can control our mind and then find expression in our behavior.

Mind of Peacemaking:
We can cultivate a mind of peacemaking through meditation, empathy, ethics, compassion, wisdom, moving beyond ego,

experiencing unity, and manifesting generosity, equanimity, and trust. Exemplars of the mind of peacemaking include His Holiness (HH) the 14th Dalai Lama. Methods of fostering a mind of peacemaking include meditation and ethical practice. But this is never easy. Where do you struggle with letting go of negative emotions? (pause) Share with the person next to you. (five minutes)

In the words of HH the 14th Dalai Lama: "Many people today agree that we need to reduce violence in our society. If we are truly serious about this, we must deal with the roots of violence, particularly those that exist within each of us. We need to embrace 'inner disarmament,' reducing our own emotions of suspicion, hatred, and hostility toward our brothers and sisters."

Behavior (Individual/Exterior)

Behavior of Warmongering:
Violent, harmful behaviors include acts of superiority or hatred toward other races or women or different sexual and gender orientations, as well as greed, consumerism, corruption, meat eating, being part of a throwaway society, and packing a gun.

Behavior of Peacemaking
We can cultivate the behavior of peacemaking through practicing happiness, non-violence, facilitative leadership, collaboration, compassionate action, reconciliation, mediation, vegetarianism, promoting diversity, and care for environmental sustainability. Exemplars of the behavior of peacemaking include Martin Luther King Jr., Mahatma Gandhi, and Peace

Pilgrim who walked across America for 28 years. Malala has said "I would not shoot someone threatening me." Methods of behavioral peacemaking include non-violent resistance and group facilitation. But, this is never easy. How do you struggle to manage your harmful behavior? (pause) Share with a person next to you how you struggle with this. (five minutes)

Culture (Collective/Interior)

Culture of Warmongering:
Violent, harmful cultures emerge from stories, symbols, and rituals of racism, sexism, intolerance, nationalism, classism, ageism, and homophobia.

Culture of Peacemaking
We can catalyze a culture of peacemaking by living by principles of sustainability, justice, equality, participation, and tolerance. We can create new stories, songs, symbols, and rites that embody these principles. On March 1st, a Climate March began to traverse the USA which includes my colleague David Zahrt along with many others. But, it is never easy to manifest new cultural forms. Where do you struggle to do this? (pause) Share with someone near you.

Systems (Collective/Exterior)

Systems of Warmongering:
Violent, harmful systems are manifestations of collective greed, fear, anger, hatred or pride including exorbitant

wealth accumulation, militarism, armed conflict, maintaining armed forces, the armaments industry, nuclear proliferation, capital punishment, the extraction, selling and burning of fossil fuels, plutocracy and systemic poverty, injustice and inequality.

Systems of Peacemaking
We can cultivate new systems of peacemaking by creating policies and institutions that promote environmental sustainability, renewable energy, socio-economic justice, gender equality, participatory governance, cultural tolerance, nuclear disarmament, an end to capital punishment, delegitimized war, and universal education and health care. Exemplars of creating systems of peacemaking include Nelson Mandela and Bill McKibben of 350.org. But, any of this is not easy. Where do you struggle to challenge the present corrupt systems and catalyze new systems of justice? (pause) Share with someone near you. (five minutes)

Conclusion:
Creative peacemaking can begin in any of the four quadrants. We can teach meditation, practice non-violent networking, or advocate new stories or new policies. Wherever we begin, we can affect the other quadrants. We can also design projects that activate all four quadrants.

Most of us could agree with these faces of peacemaking, but what is blocking us, what is keeping this from happening, what do we need to do to do this? I struggle to do these things. What are your struggles? We need a balance between patience and consideration and urgency and boldness. How can we do this? It is not easy. It is incredibly challenging. It can be boring. It is hard work. Its outcome is uncertain. It will not make us rich or popular. How do we move forward day after day? (pause)

Who is drawn to help nurture the mind of peacemaking? The behavior of peacemaking? The culture of peacemaking? Systems and policies of peacemaking? All four dimensions?

STRATEGIES, PARTNERSHIPS AND PROJECTS

Introduction:
Over the next two days, we can design creative initiatives and projects of education, networking, and advocacy.

Education
We can design educational projects to promote creative peacemaking. These can involve teaching meditation or ethics and providing relevant information. They can teach non-violent resistance, facilitation, mediation, new stories of dialogue and justice and new policy messages. Who is already working in this area? Who wants to work in this area?

Networking
We can also design networking projects that promote collaboration and group facilitation. We can promote networking among diverse communities to nurture understanding, among facilitators and mediators, among new exemplars of peacemaking, and among policy makers. Who is working in this field? Who would like to work on this?

Advocacy

We can also design projects that advocate for new mind-sets, individual behaviors, new cultural expressions, or new policies and institutions of peacemaking. These can involve speaking out, writing, blogging, creating artforms, and political engagement. Who is already doing any of these? Who would like to work on any of these?

Who is drawn to work primarily on educational initiatives? Networking initiatives? Advocacy initiatives? All three?

Conclusion:

This symposium can invent creative new pathways to peace, new language, new methods, new partnerships, new projects, new ideas, new rituals, and new policies.

Let us conclude with a dance that will allow us to further embody and internalize the four movements of peacemaking: "Dance of the Peacemakers" (to Pachelbel's Canon) in concentric circles

CLOSING AND CHARGE

My challenge to you over the next two days and for the rest of your life is to push for breakthrough thinking towards radical being and doing. Speak your truth. Listen to other's truth. Risk bold proposals. Manifest your ground of values. Dare to be the change that the world needs.

Let us end with a responsive ritual which we will repeat three times: Me: These are the Times! You: We are the People!

May all people everywhere, including you and me, realize peace, happiness, understanding and compassion.

8

"Collaborative Leadership in a Time of Whole System Transformation"

UN Public Service Awards and Global Forum 2014

Seoul, Republic of Korea
23 – 26 June 2014

A little over three months later, I travelled to Seoul to give the eighth critical decade call to action. The context was the annual UN global forum on public service with the theme "Innovating Governance for Sustainable Development and Well-being of the People." My talk was about collaborative governance in a time of whole system transformation. I also facilitated a workshop demonstrating methods of collaborative decision-making. I was grateful to be back in the country where I had lived and worked for five years, where both my sons were born, and where I have several close colleagues.

From Serving People & Planet: *"At the invitation of Dr. Adriana Alberti, in June, I facilitated a workshop in Seoul, South Korea, on e-governance and made a presentation at the global UN Forum on Public Service and Sustainable Development. My talk was about collaborative governance and is on the internet. After the UN conference in Seoul, I had a wonderful reunion with dear friends. Rev. Dr. Kang Byoung Hoon came to my hotel for a meal and conversation. I attended a church service at Bo Moon Methodist Church in Seoul, where Rev. Dr. Park Si Won's son Rev. Park Chul Hyun is pastor. There I got to meet Park So Hyun, Rev. Park's daughter who is a famous, German-trained organist and music professor, and the lovely grandchildren of Rev. Park and his wife Mrs. Lee Jung Ja. Rev. Park and his son also drove me out to Kuh Du I Ri, a village just south of the demilitarized zone, where his family and mine had conducted a village development project in the ICA days. The village was totally transformed as is all of Korea—so many wonderful memories." (pages 195 – 196)*

It is wonderful to be back again in Seoul where I first worked with an NGO (the Institute of Cultural Affairs) in the 1970s on community development in collaboration with Sae Maul Undong (the government's new village movement). I am happy to be here among government and civil society officials committed to public service for sustainable development. We each know the challenges we face, but let me say it this way:

You and I are living in the most critical moment in human history, a time of whole system transformation. Every natural and social system is in grave danger and requires urgent and innovative solutions and actions. Our planetary ecosystems of air, water, land, plants, and animals are in rapid degradation due to the release of carbon into the atmosphere from the burning of fossil fuels and the impacts of an ever-expanding human population. This is resulting in global warming, rapid melting of ice, sea level rise, submerging of islands and coastlines, a dramatic increase of devastating mega storms, desertification, food production collapse, and critical water shortages, and can result in social chaos and much more.

And if this were not enough, at the same time we face long-standing gender inequality, massive socio-economic injustice, elitist governance institutions, and widespread cultural and religious intolerance. It is my heartfelt belief that these crises present us with an unparalleled opportunity to turn civilization itself in the direction of compassion and sustainability. And if we fail to do so, we will pay the price – a degraded planet and social misery.

But, we can commit ourselves to collaborative action to create gender equality, socio-economic justice, participatory governance, and cultural tolerance. Innovative solutions and actions are urgently needed at every level of government, industry, and civil society to respond to these multiple, interlocking crises. To achieve innovative solutions and effective actions new kinds of collaboration among these three governance actors are needed as well as collaboration among government agencies themselves, among NGOs, among corporations, and among the individuals within each of these.

Earlier this year, I was teaching a seminar on collaborative leadership at the University of Aruba with Dr. Juliet Chieuw, who you will hear from tomorrow. Suddenly, I became aware that the major challenge of collaboration is that it involves other people! Working with other people is never easy but is essential to the success of the human enterprise. Let us briefly explore the concepts and practice of collaboration, leadership, methods of collaborative leadership, and how it is essential to our survival as a species.

What is collaboration? Collaboration involves teamwork, the promotion of synergy and creating collective intelligence, mutual respect, trust, and learning. It involves honoring diverse perspectives and gifts, moving beyond one own ego, achieving common vision and values and self-organization. One of my favorite examples of this is within the private sector. To invent the Visa card, Dee Hock had a group of diverse individuals work together with only two things in common – a shared vision and shared values. Out of their collaboration emerged the design of the Visa card based on the collaboration of competing businesses who were committed to using the Visa card for business transactions.

And as for us, I believe our common vision is sustainable human development, or what I have identified as an emerging civilization of compassion. And, I believe that our common values include not only sustainability but equality, justice, participation, and tolerance. But, we must invite everyone to participate in this brainstorming on vision and values.

What is leadership? Leadership has developmental phases including the authoritative, the bureaucratic, and the pragmatic. It can also evolve into participatory, facilitative, creative, system-wide, interactive, adaptive, and transformative leadership. Group facilitation is a great example of this new style of leadership. In this form of leadership, the facilitator asks question after question to help a group of people identify their shared vision, obstacles, strategies, and action plans. By honoring individual brainstorming, collective grouping of data and naming of clusters of data, a group of people can collaborate in creating a strategic plan that they own because they created it. And, they are motivated to carry out the plan because it is their own, as individuals and as a group. In this workshop, we are using participatory methods that allow everyone in the room to create our recommended actions.

What then is collaborative leadership? Collaborative leadership is a dynamic, creative, self-organizing team of orchestrated, diverse perspectives and gifts driven by common vision and values. To launch a rocket into space many technicians much collaborate intimately. The entire enterprise of science itself requires careful collaboration among many scientists around the globe. A choreographer must collaborate with the dancers to produce a great work of art. Architects of communal spaces must collaborate with the public to design workable solutions. Within whole-of-government, collaborative leadership is the commitment to honoring every individual and every ministry and agencies' insights and knowledge in the creation of open, transparent, and accountable governance systems responsive to the voices and priorities of every citizen, especially the most vulnerable.

Why then is collaborative leadership essential in whole-of-government?

This critical moment of history requires everyone's participation and collaboration. How otherwise can nations and communities respond to the multiple crises we face without effective collaboration? Everyone's perspective and energy in every government agency is needed in a concerted effort. Every NGO and business must be involved. And, all of these must be working harmoniously together in a common cause. Finally, the intelligence and energy of 7.3 billion people must be mobilized and orchestrated with common vision and values in seamless action.

What are some of the most effective methods and applications of collaborative leadership? The most effective methods of collaborative leadership that I am aware of include group facilitation (such as the Technology of Participation, Appreciative Inquiry and Open Space), use of integral frameworks addressing individual mindsets and behaviors and collective cultures and institutions, social artistry processes that enhance sensory, psychological, symbolic and unitive experience, as well as systems thinking, strategic planning, effective team building, and peer learning-by-doing.

Tomorrow you will hear an excellent example of some of these approaches incorporated in a University of Aruba training program. This innovative, powerful program equips educational administrators to foster collaboration among teachers, students, parents, administrators, local community, government, private sector, and NGOs led by a compelling vision of Aruba as an Enlightened Society.

Collaboration is not only worth the effort. It has become a necessity if we humans are to enjoy sustainable human development on a healthy planet.

9

"21st Century Leadership as Global Citizens and World Servers"

Horace Mann School, The Recital Hall

New York City
22 October 2015

*F*ive months later, I gave the ninth critical decade talk back in New York City. This was for the students, faculty, administrators, and parents of an elite, private school. Following the talk, I facilitated a workshop. This is the first time I talked about an emerging civilization of* compassion. *I also expounded on the movement of movements (MoM), and the methods and processes of innovative leadership.*

From Serving People & Planet: *"In October at Horace Mann School (HMS), an elite private school in New York City,*

I gave a lecture and workshop to its very bright students, dedicated faculty, and devoted parents on global citizenship, visionary leadership, and sustainable development. This was at the invitation of social artistry colleague Karen Johnson, photography teacher at HMS." (page 198)

Opening

Thank you, Karen Johnson. Great work, Social Artistry Team! Thanks to you and Dr. Kelly for inviting me to be with you today. And, good afternoon, students, parents, teachers, and administrators of Horace Mann School. (show of hands for each of the four groups) Please introduce yourself to people around you – your name and what you hope will happen in the next hour and its follow up.

My name is Robertson Work. I have worked in international development for 45 years in 55 countries – first at the grassroots project level helping poor communities as part of an NGO, the Institute of Cultural Affairs, then at the global policy level with the UN Development Programme helping countries in the field of decentralized governance, and now at the individual educational level teaching innovative leadership at NYU Wagner Graduate School of Public Service here in New York City.

I hope that in this session you and I can think together about what is happening in our world and what we are called to know, do and be today and in the years ahead. I have studied your website, been to the Dorr Nature Laboratory, visited the clubs and publications membership fair, had a campus site visit, and have just held a meeting with some of the club members. I must confess that I am impressed with who you are, what you are doing here at Horace Mann, and the huge potential you have for making a positive impact on the world.

You are committed to leading "great and giving lives." You are committed to truth, the life of the mind, mature behavior, mutual respect, creating a secure and healthful environment, and maintaining balance between individual achievement and a caring community. You are committed to sustainability, diversity, and service to others. I salute you, your mission, and your core values. And, I believe that those to whom much is given, much is called forth. And to those driven by high aspirations, lives of great service are possible.

What is a global citizen? We are all Earthlings, evolving from the Earth, part of the Earth and stewards of the Earth. "I am a citizen of the world", wrote Diogenes Laertius, Greek philosopher (AD 220). "The world is my country, all [humankind] are my [sisters and brothers], and to do good is my religion", wrote Thomas Paine, American revolutionary (AD 1776). I was born in a small town in Oklahoma, went around the Earth at twenty-four and fell in love with her and her Earthlings. Who has traveled to other countries? Who has lived in other countries? Who was born in another country? But I say to you, anyone in any circumstance can be a global citizen. Were any of you at the Global Citizen Festival in Central Park recently? Check out the website: http://globalcitizen.org

Let us begin with a few minutes of stillness and "seconds of silence" to relax and become fully present, here, and now. (3 min. of mindfulness)

Turn to someone near you and share in one minute each what you are most concerned about in the world today. (3 min. of buzz) Okay, anyone: what did the other person say?

Let's spend the next several minutes thinking together about our times of crisis and opportunity, a vision of a new civilization, the movement of movements that can take us there and the innovative leadership and sustaining practices that will be required. As I speak let your minds dialogue with what I am saying: what did he say? how did it make me feel? what did it remind me of? what does it mean to me? what is my decision about this? and what will I do about it?).

I. **Our Times of Crisis and Opportunity** (Image: glacier falling into the sea)
We are living in the most critical time in all human history. Why do I say that? Never in the past 5,000 years have we faced such colossal danger and such exhilarating possibility. We are the brink of either mass extinction or a whole new way of being human on planet Earth. Which it will be depends on what you and I do with our lives. Thus, our being together this afternoon.

A. Climate Chaos and Degradation of Ecosystems
Climate chaos and degradation of ecosystems are upon us. We thought fossil fuels were a brilliant solution for our energy needs. It turns out that they have been destroying our life support systems of air, water, ice, soil, plants, and animals. This is because of the release of carbon dioxide

from the extraction and burning of coal, oil and natural gas. Carbon dioxide and other greenhouse gases released into the atmosphere are warming the planet and melting the ice around the planet, causing sea levels to rise, flooding coastal areas, and will submerge many islands. In addition, global warming is causing mega-storms and wild fires, desertification and water shortages, collapse of food production, loss of biodiversity (the sixth extinction) and acidification of the oceans, and could result in human mass migrations, and social and economic volatility. I remind you of this not to frighten you, but to sound the alarm that we must and can change our ways right now.

B.   Patriarchy and Misogyny

For thousands of years it has been understood that men are dominant and should control and lead women. This view is called patriarchy and has been strengthened by the world's religions which predominately have male gods, male saviors, and male priests. Some men fear and even hate women. This is called misogyny. The problems with these views in addition to their doing harm to women is that they have kept women from exercising their rightful leadership in society at all levels. Without honoring women's views, knowledge and wisdom, societies have become overly masculinized with the destruction of the natural world and the promotion of militarization, win-lose competition, and a culture of violence. I remind you of this not to frighten you but to sound the alarm that we must and can change our ways right now.

C.   Oligarchy, Plutocracy and Corporatocracy

Even though democracy has been around for over three hundred years, we see today that democratic elections and representation around the world have been greatly weakened by a few powerful entities and people. Did you know, for example, that only 158 families have provided half of the money supporting presidential candidates for the 2016 US elections? When a few families control a country, it is called an oligarchy. When a few wealthy people control a country, it is called a plutocracy. Corporations are controlling elections, legislation, and the mass media to control society. This is called corporatocracy. One of the problems with this trend is that the needs, voices and wisdom of poor and middle-class people are being ignored, and they are suffering. I remind you of this not to worry or frighten you, but to sound the alarm that we must and can change our ways right now.

D.   Systemic Poverty and Social Deprivation

2.5 billion people live on less than $2 per day. 2.6 billion lack access to sanitation. 1 billion have no access to safe water. 10 million preventable child deaths occur each year. We cannot escape old age, sickness, and death, but we can relieve our suffering in so many ways. In the past 30 years income inequality has skyrocketed. One percent of the world's population owns 50% of the world's wealth. And, in the US, the top one percent owns as much wealth as the bottom 90%. The number of poor people has expanded, and the middle class has been significantly weakened. Most people do not have adequate income or access to quality education and health services. This is because the economic system based on accumulation and greed is designed to favor the wealthy. If you have money you can make money with money. If you do not have money you have to work for wages that are often inadequate to support you and your family. One of the many problems with this situation is that most people are suffering and do not see how they can sustain their lives. I remind you of this not to make you feel guilty but to sound the alarm that we must and can change our ways right now.

E. Prejudice, Nationalism and Militarism

People who are different are often looked down on and often harmed. This includes people of different races, ethnic groups, religions, economic classes, and sexual orientations. This of course is called bias or prejudice. People in different countries are often feared and attacked with massive use of armaments. This is militarism. People think that their country is always right and is the only one that is important. This is called nationalism. These views are based on ignorance, fear, and hatred. The problem with these views is that they cause many people to suffer. I remind you of this not to make you sad, but to sound the alarm that we must and can change and help others change their views and behavior.

F. Command-and-Control Leadership

Today the dominant style of leadership is command-and-control. The leader is seen as superior and to be obeyed. He is usually male. Leadership is seen to be about strength, authority, and control of others. One of the problems with this approach to leadership is that it does not seek or value the views, intelligence, and participation of other people. It is therefore less intelligent and does not reflect the ideas and needs of other people and causes them harm. I remind you of this not to make you angry or depressed, but to sound the alarm that we must and can change and help others change their views and behavior.

II. A Vision of a New Civilization of Compassion

Yes, a global citizen needs to be clear on these crises, problems, and challenges, but we also need to dream of a new world that is so attractive that it beckons us and motivates us to create it. What are your greatest hopes for the future? What is indeed possible? What is necessary? What would a new civilization of compassion look like? Remember, compassion is not only feeling someone else's pain but is vowing to relieve their suffering.

Compassion in the first instance is not religious or even spiritual. It is a natural response of living beings who have empathy for each other and want to help each other. Parents are one of the best examples of compassion. A parent will do anything to help relieve the suffering of their children and to help them be happy. A compassionate civilization is the universalization of this quality of compassion directed toward all beings everywhere. Or, it can be called love, or care, or being neighborly, or helpful.

What might a new civilization of compassion look like? It will be based on six principles: sustainability, equality, justice, participation, tolerance, and nonviolence.

A.   Environmental Sustainability

The new civilization of compassion will embody environmental sustainability at its very core. As Naomi Klein says:
"Climate change isn't just a crisis. It's a chance to build a better world." People will realize that there can be no human
life without healthy ecosystems of air, water, soil, plants,
and animals. We will keep the remaining fossil fuels in the
ground. All energy will be from renewable sources such as
sun, wind, water, geothermal and algae. We will protect the
natural environment. The new economy will be 100% environmentally friendly.

B.   Gender Equality

A compassionate civilization will embody gender equality
in every facet of human society. Women will be leaders at
every level of society. Women will be paid the same as men
for the same work. The voices, views and wisdom of women
will be honored and celebrated. Men will respect and protect the sovereignty of women's bodies and minds. Gender
and sexual orientation will be understood and accepted as
taking a multiplicity of forms.

C.   Participatory Governance

A compassionate civilization will embody participatory governance. The needs, voices, views, and wisdom of all people will set the policy agendas for society
through new processes and institutions of direct democracy. This will include face-to-face and online policy
dialogue.

D. Socio-economic Justice

A compassionate civilization will embody socio-economic justice. Everyone will have meaningful engagement, adequate income and access to high quality education and health services.

E. Cultural Tolerance

A compassionate civilization will embody cultural tolerance. It will be understood and accepted that all people of every race, ethnic background, religion, economic class, and nationality should be respected and free to exercise their rights as human beings. People will enjoy learning from others who have a different background and orientation to life.

F. Innovative Leadership

A compassionate civilization will embody innovative leadership. Leadership will have evolved beyond the authoritative, bureaucratic, and pragmatic to principled leadership honoring multiple perspectives. Leadership will be understood as an art of human behavior and interaction that can be practiced by anyone in any position. Leadership will be facilitative, participatory, inspiring, systemic, and creative.

At this point you may be saying to yourself, but all sounds utopian. Is it possible to achieve? I would say to you that if we do not head for utopia we will be left in endless dystopia of environmental degradation and social misery. Let's go for it!

III. The Movement of Movements

How will we get from our current situation of crisis to a new civilization of compassion? Fortunately, there are already many forces moving us in that direction. These are the many movements that each promote a vision. If they can work together, these movements will become a powerful movement of movements (MoM) that will help humanity realize its full potential.

A. Environmental, Climate and Green Energy Movements

There are the environmental, climate, and green energy movements. The environmental movement is committed to protecting the natural environment. The climate movement is motivated to help us mitigate and adapt to climate chaos. The green energy movement is promoting the rapid transition to an energy system of 100% renewable energy from sun, wind, water, geothermal and algae. This includes networks and organizations such as 350.org, Greenpeace and Transition Towns.

B. Women's and LGBTQ Movements

We also have the women's movement and the LGBTQ movement. The women's movement promotes the rights, voice, leadership, and protection of women. Women gained the right to vote only 95 years ago and must be paid the same as men for the same work. The LGBTQ movement is concerned about the safety and freedom of LGBTQ youth and adults. Groups in these movements include the National

Organization of Women (NOW) and International Gay and Lesbian Human Rights Commission and others.

C.   Direct Democracy and Decentralization Movements
Then there are the direct democracy movement and the decentralization movement. The direct democracy movement promotes the formation of new democratic processes and institutions that allow the views and needs of citizen to be the basis for policy formulation. The decentralization movement helps move power, decision making, and service delivery beyond national and state capitals to towns and villages throughout a country.

D.   Labor Union and Post-Capitalism Movements
There are also the labor union movement and the post-capitalism movement. The labor movement helps workers organize into unions that can negotiate their salaries and benefits so that they are not taken advantage of by management. The post-capitalism movement is promoting the creation of a new economic system that values the wellbeing of all the people and all of nature over profits for a small elite.

E.   Human Rights and Peace Movements
We also have the human rights movement and the peace movement. The human rights movement is committed to realizing the Universal Declaration of Human Rights for every women, man, and child. The peace movement is working hard to promote nonviolence, diplomacy, and negotiation, to stop wars and to delegitimize war as an acceptable

manner for resolving conflict. As written on the Horace Mann School peace poles: "May peace prevail in our hearts, in our communities, in our nations and on the Earth."

F.   Group Facilitation and Social Artistry Movements

Finally, there is the facilitation movement and the social artistry movement. The facilitation movement is promoting the power of group facilitation to involve all of the people of an organization or community in its own decision making. This includes the IAF – the International Association of Facilitators, and the ToP Network – the Technology of Participation, created by the Institute of Cultural Affairs (ICA). This week is International Facilitation Week celebrating the power of group facilitation. The social artistry movement trains educators and leaders in organizations and communities to enhance people's creativity and passion in ways that create a world that works for all. This includes the work of the Jean Houston Foundation and the training that Karen Johnson, Woody and Denise and their team are doing here at Horace Mann. (Who has been part of any of their events?)

Of course, there are many other movements as well. The point is that when these movements work together, they are unstoppable. They can and will create a new civilization of compassion. The UN is among those at the forefront of this movement of movements. Last month the 193 countries of the UN launched 17 sustainable development goals (SDGs) for 2030. The UN has also just released a new series of action comics of superheroes who help achieve the goals. How are we each a superhero as a global citizen and world server in this historic moment? Achieving these goals will take us a long way towards a new civilization of compassion. Many of your clubs are already working on one or more of these goals.

Which movement is your favorite? Which one are you already part of? Which one do you want to become part of?

IV. Innovative Leadership and Self Sustenance

To move from our time of crisis towards a new civilization of compassion, we need to provide innovative leadership of the movement of movements (MoM) and in government, corporations, NGOs, academia, and media. There are many methods of effective and innovative leadership. I would like to share four that I have found to be particularly powerful. They are 1) integral systems thinking, 2) group facilitation and participatory planning, 3) social artistry, and 4) mindfulness, ethics, and servant-leadership.

A.   Integral Systems Thinking (4 Quadrants)

The innovative leader engages in integral systems thinking in four dimensions – the interior (consciousness) and exterior (the material world) and the individual and collective. By analyzing and planning within four quadrants at the intersection of these dimensions, the innovative leader is aware of and is addressing all aspects of any issue or situation. She/he knows that every situation has an interior-individual dimension, an exterior-individual dimension, an interior-collective dimension, and an exterior-collective dimension. The interior-individual dimension includes people's mindsets, attitudes, values, and assumptions which as a leader you must be aware of and help evolve. The exterior-individual dimension includes people's behaviors, speech, and interpersonal relations that need new skillful means. The interior-collective dimension includes culture, myths, symbols, rituals, and norms that influence people some of which need to be transformed. The exterior-collective dimension includes systems, policies, institutions, organizations, and communities that need to continually evolve. For example, in dealing with climate change the innovative leader must employ strategies to change individual mindsets and behavior as well as collective culture and systems. When at the UN, I used integral systems thinking to help design new policies and programs.

B.   Group Facilitation and Participatory Planning (ToP)
The innovative leader uses group facilitation techniques and processes to enable people to engage in participatory conversations and planning. The facilitator asks question after question provoking the best thinking and cooperation of the group. For example, in the ToP (Technology of Participation) methodology, the innovative leader facilitates group conversations in a four-part sequence called ORID: Objective, Reflective, Interpretive, and Decisional. This allows the group to go from an objective appreciation (what do you notice?), to delve into emotions and memory (how do you feel about it or what does it remind you of?), to telling a story or identifying the meaning (what is the significance?), and finally to making a decision concerning what actions

are needed (what is your decision?). In participatory strategic planning, the facilitator leads the group in 1) articulat-
ing their future Vision, 2) analyzing current Obstacles to the
vision, 3) creating Strategies to deal with the obstacles and
move toward the vision, and 4) deciding on Actions and a
timeline for realizing the strategies. This week, I am facilitating an online conversation on the power of facilitation using
the ORID method. When I was in UNDP, I used the participatory strategic planning method to develop policies and projects around the world.

C.   Social Artistry (SA)

The innovative leader uses social artistry techniques and processes to enhance people's creativity and commitment. The
social artist enables people to become aware and involved
in social change on four levels: sensory/physical, psychologi-
cal/historical, mythic/symbolic, and unitive/integral. At the
sensory/physical level people deepen their awareness of
the physical situation using their five senses. At the psycho-
logical/historical level people look at their memories, feelings, and associations. At the mythic/symbolic level people
explore the stories and symbols that give meaning to their
lives, and they also create new stories concerning new pos-
sibilities. And at the unitive/integral level, people experience unity or at-oneness with the group or reality that they
are dealing with. If the social artist can expand and deepen
people's awareness at these four levels, there is greater like-
lihood of achieving breakthrough, creative, inspiring, and
lasting change. When I was in UNDP, I helped train people

in several countries in social artistry so that could be more effective in decentralizing the MDGs in their countries by enhancing their human capacities.

D.   Mindfulness, Ethics and Servant Leadership

The innovative leader uses mindfulness exercises and ethical practices to call people to a profound sense of being servant-leaders. Mindfulness exercises include relaxation, meditation, and contemplation. By enhancing and deepening their awareness, people gain detached engagement, understanding, compassion, and wisdom. Ethical study and practice help people live lives based on their deepest values and principles such as compassion, truth, justice, equality, and understanding. Learning to be a servant-leader is a lifelong journey of letting go of one's ego and focusing ones energies on helping and serving others. In the words of Horace Mann School: living great and giving lives. I meditate daily and teach my NYU grad students in all four of the above leadership methods.

These four approaches to innovative leadership, among others, are needed to propel organizations, movements, and the movement of movements toward the realization of a compassionate civilization. These innovative leadership methods can be learned, practiced, and applied right here at Horace Mann, in the Bronx community, in New York City, in New York State, throughout the USA, and around the world.

Closing

You at Horace Mann School are committed to truth, to service, to sustainability, and to diversity. As such you can embrace the truth of our time of crisis and opportunity, the need to build a sustainable society that honors diversity, and the necessity of leading great and giving lives of individual and collective service. You can embody this in your curriculum, your individual and institutional behavior and environment, your clubs, and publications, and in your action projects. You – students, parents, teachers, and administrators – are called to do much good in this suffering world as global citizens, world servers, and innovative leaders.

What you tell yourself about what you are doing is crucial. This reminds me of a story of three stone cutters somewhere in medieval Europe. A stranger asked one of them, what are you doing? The stonecutter said, I am chipping away at the stone. He asked the second stone cutter, what are you doing? The stonecutter said, I am feeding my family. Then the stranger asked the third stonecutter, what are you doing? He took a deep breath, looked up at the stranger, and said with dignity: sir, I am building a cathedral. What is your and my life about? What is your story? What motivates you to do what you do? Are you just doing a job or are you building a compassionate civilization?

As students, you can commit yourself to create a better world right now and throughout your life. You can vow to be a global citizen. You can prepare yourself for a life of service as an innovative leader. You can develop the skills needed to create breakthroughs in society on behalf of the least, the last, and the lost. You can study and play hard and become a good human being who inspires others to be the best that they can be. Some of you will decide to spend your lives promoting environmental sustainability, or gender equality, or participatory governance, or socio-economic justice, or cultural tolerance and understanding. Some of you will take on all of it!

As parents you can support your children in their self-realization of living great and giving lives. You can yourselves do all that you can to create a world that is sustainable, equitable, just, participatory, tolerant, and peaceful.

As teachers you can bring the exploration of these crises, visions, movements, and leadership approaches into your curriculum. You can model for your students what it means to be an innovative leader who is building a better world. When you relate to your students as present and future innovative leaders, you can hold a vision of their doing remarkable things as global citizens and world servers.

As administrators you can continue to create an institution of excellence not only in scholarship but in service, sustainability, and diversity.

What would Horace Mann himself say to us today? "Let us not be content to wait to see what will happen but give us the determination to make the right things to happen."

And "If any [person] seeks for greatness, let [her/]him forget greatness and ask for truth, and [she/]he will find both."

I would like to conclude with words of the English poet D.H. Lawrence written in 1916, yet for this very moment:

Not I, not I, but the wind that blows through me!
A fine wind is blowing the new direction of Time.
If only I let it bear me, carry me, if only it carry me!

If only I am sensitive, subtle, oh, delicate, a winged gift!
If only, most lovely of all I yield myself and am borrowed
By the fine, fine wind that takes its course through the chaos of the world
Like a fine, an exquisite chisel, a wedge-blade inserted;
If only I am keen and hard like the sheer tip of a wedge
Driven by invisible blows,
The rock will split, we shall come at the wonder, we shall find the Hesperides [a new civilization, a new world, new leadership].
Oh, for the wonder that bubbles into my soul,
I would be a good fountain, a good well-head,
Would blur no whisper, spoil no expression.
What is the knocking?
What is the knocking at the door in the night?
It is somebody wants to do us harm.
No, no, it is the three strange angels.
Admit them, admit them.
("Song of a Man Who Has Come Through")

Please repeat after me the powerful words of the paleontologist, theologian Pierre Teilhard de Chardin:

The task before us now
If we would not perish
Is to shake off our ancient prejudices
And to build the Earth

Let's do it!

10
"Compassionate Communities"

World Fair Field Festival and International Day of Peace Symposium

Fairfield Arts and Convention Center, Fairfield, Iowa, USA
21 September 2018

The tenth critical decade call to action was given in Fairfield, Iowa, for students and faculty from nearby schools and universities, and town residents. The event was a symposium marking the international day of peace. This was one year after I published my book A Compassionate Civilization: The Urgency of Sustainable Development and Mindful Activism.

From Serving People & Planet*: "In September, I promoted the messages of* A Compassionate Civilization *by giving the keynote address on the International Day of Peace at the World Fair Field Festival and Symposium in Fairfield, Iowa. My nephew Matthew Lindberg-Work had told the World Fair*

Field organizers, Kaye Jacobs and Richard Beall, leaders of a private school at the Maharishi University of Management (MUM), about my UN career and my new book, and the organizers invited me to give the keynote. I had been in Fairfield several years prior when my nephew had received his undergraduate degree from the Maharishi University. Matthew had then taught chemistry at MUM. Duncan and Lisa [my brother and sister-in-law] visited Fairfield whenever they could, as they were both trained Transcendental Meditation (TM) teachers and practitioners. I enjoyed being back in Fairfield, meeting so many fine people and participating in the symposium and the festival in the town square. People were very kind throughout my stay there. And, I got to meet Kesha Nelson, Matthew's fiancée. What a great lady. Welcome to the family, Kesha! Later, I commissioned a "Compassionate Communities" video produced by Werner Elmker based on the film he took of my keynote in Fairfield. (It is on the internet.)" (pages 213 – 214)

May all beings everywhere realize peace, happiness, wisdom, and compassion. Greetings on this beautiful day, the International Day of Peace. Peace in society is built on sustainable development; and sustainable development is built on peace in society.

Please enjoy a moment of silence, stillness, and awareness – peace inner and outer. Please close your eyes or lower your gaze aware of being here, being now. (pause)

Thank you, Richard Beall, Kaye Jacob, Karen, and everyone on the organizing team, volunteers, and sponsors. Would you please stand.

I am happy to be with you today and tomorrow for this amazing event that is a model for other communities across Iowa, the USA, and the world.

Did you know that Fairfield was a trading center with indigenous people before it became an incorporated town? That it hosted the first Iowa State Fair 164 years ago in 1854, thus the "field for the fair"? That it took part in the underground railroad to help former slaves flee the South? That it held Hometown Shows far and wide during the Depression after the Stewart brothers started the Universal Producing Co.? And, that it now has the largest group of yogic flyers in the world, and is full of artists, authors, entrepreneurs, and eighty cultures! Wow. The "fair" in Fairfield also means beautiful or just; and a "field" is a meadow, an area, an arena, or an energy matrix. Therefore, "Fairfield" is also a Beautiful and Just Meadow and Arena of Positive, World Changing Energy where compassion can take root and grow and blossom around the planet. I grew up in a town the size of Fairfield and have done community and organizational development in 55 countries. I know that transformation can take root in one local community and spread around the planet.

I came to this beautiful, energetic meadow once before for the graduation of my nephew Matthew Lindberg-Work at MIU's undergrad school. Matthew and fiancée Kesha please stand up. Matthew's parents, my brother Duncan Work and sister-in-law Lisa Lindberg come here often for TM (Transcendental Meditation) events and have many friends here.

As you probably know, imagination is a powerful force. If we can imagine something, we can often create it.

Please close your eyes: what are your greatest hopes and dreams for Fairfield or your town by the year 2028? Imagine with your mind's eye that it is now 2028 and Fairfield or your town has achieved your greatest hopes and dreams. What do you see, hear, feel? (pause) Now turn to another person and share your visions of 2028 Fairfield or your town in one minute each.

This morning, I invite you to think with each other and with me about compassionate action, the crises and opportunities that we face, the principles that can guide us, the areas of transformation where we need to put our energy, and the movement of movements (MOM) that will help us create a compassionate Fairfield, Iowa, America, and world. I will ask you a question; you will talk and listen to someone near you; then I will share my thoughts; I may ask another question; and then we will move on. This will be a dialogical-interactive keynote, okay?

The word compassion is made up of "com" (with) and "passion" (suffering): to be with suffering, another's, and one's own. Compassionate action is not just a feeling; it is not simply empathy. It is decisive action that I or you or someone takes to help relieve the suffering of a living being, someone else, or yourself. I believe that compassionate action is the key to the future of life on Earth.

You and I live in the most critical time in human history. Other times thought they were it; they were wrong; this is it. We face multiple, inter-locking crises including climate chaos, patriarchy and misogyny, systemic poverty, plutocracy and corporatocracy, bigotry, and perpetual warfare. Whether we move toward utopia or dystopia is up to you, me, and all people around this planet.

Our planet is warming because of the release of carbon dioxide, methane, and other greenhouse gases from the burning of fossil fuels, the raising of animals for meat, and other human activities resulting in the melting of ice caps and glaciers, sea rise, coastal flooding, forest fires, mega storms, social dislocation, and much more. I have just come from the floods of North Carolina. Women, half of humanity, have been subjugated by men for thousands of years resulting in overly masculinized societies based on aggression and cutthroat competition. Billions of people live in poverty because of systems of colonialization, neocolonialization, and globalized capitalism. 20% of the children of Fairfield live below the poverty line. Wealthy elites and their corporations, out of endless greed, control our political and economic systems. Bias, prejudice, and bigotry are widespread due to misunderstanding, fear and hatred of people who are of a different race, ethnicity, religion, culture, or sexual orientation. And a pervasive culture of violence justifies and maintains armed conflict between and within nations and ubiquitous violence in everyday life.

These six crises are mutually causative and supportive and are demanding a whole system transformation if life on Earth is to continue and we are to thrive.

How do these crises manifest here in Fairfield or in your town? Please share with your neighbor.

For me, six principles provide the motivation and direction needed. These are: sustainability, equality, justice, participation, tolerance, and nonviolence. Sustainability is concerned with longevity, life, and healthy ecosystems. Equality is a sacred principle that every life is precious and deserves to exist and to flourish. Justice is a fierce principle of the overcoming of conditions that are unfair or harmful. Participation is concerned with enabling the voice, priorities, and wellbeing of every person in societal dialogue, and policy making and implementation. Tolerance is based on the understanding that the multitude of unique expressions of being human are each valuable and have wisdom to share with others. And, nonviolence is a sacred choice to refrain from doing harm even while holding firm to what is right and true. These six principles will carry us ever forward in our noble quest for a compassionate society.

Which of these principles or other principles are most important to you, your life, your work in the world? Please share with your neighbor.

For me, the required areas of transformation are environmental sustainability, gender equality, socioeconomic justice, participatory governance, cultural tolerance, and peace and nonviolence.

Environmental sustainability includes the cessation of extracting and burning fossil fuels, protecting biodiversity of other species of animals and plants, protecting the health of water, air, and land, the use of green energy, and mitigating and adapting to climate chaos. Seven of the UN's Sustainable Development Goals (SDGs) are in this area. Gender equality is the full partnership of women and men with the voices and wisdom of women in leadership positions at all levels of society emphasizing collaboration and caring. One SDG is in this area. Socioeconomic justice includes the provision of quality healthcare, education, and a livable wage and universal basic income for all people. Six SDGs are in this area. Participatory governance is radical, direct democracy in which every person's voice, vote, and priorities are a determining force in the political process. One SDG is related to this area. Cultural tolerance includes acceptance and appreciation of differences of religion, ethnicity, race, and culture. One SDG is in this area. And, nonviolence and peace create a world in which armed conflict has lost its legitimacy as a means of dispute resolution in favor of peaceful coexistence and cooperation and nonviolence becomes a way of life. One SDG is in this area.

These six areas of transformation are mutually supportive in creating a compassionate community and civilization. For each of these, we need to identify and articulate the hoped for future vision, the obstacles blocking that vision, strategic directions that will overcome the obstacles and move toward the vision, and the action plan and timeline that will achieve the strategies. The Technology of Participation (ToP) and other methods provide this strategic planning process and facilitative methods for planning and implementation. One of the programs I managed at UNDP was on Decentralizing the MDGs (the precursor of the SDGs) through Innovative Leadership. That is one reason why I am so excited about what Fairfield and the other Iowa towns are committing themselves to do – to localize the global SDGs at the community level.

Turn to your neighbor and discuss which of these areas of transformation are being worked on in Fairfield or in your town or needs to be worked on.

Millions of people of good will, and their organizations comprise movements that are catalyzing a better world for all. These movements include the environmental movement, the women's movement, the social justice movement, the democracy movement, the human rights movement, and the peace movement. Taken together they comprise a massive movement of movements or MOM that is transforming our world for the better. The environmental movement includes organizations such as 350.org, Transition Towns, and Green Peace. The women's movement is made up of many organizations such as NOW and Women for Justice. The social justice movement includes organizations such as labor unions. The democracy movement includes organizations such as Indivisible, Our Revolution, MoveOn, and Democracy Spring. The human rights movement includes organizations such as the ACLU, LGBTQ rights organizations, and Human Rights Watch. And, the peace movement includes many organizations that promote nonviolence, and disarmament, and call for an end to the use of armed conflict. People everywhere are waking up and standing up. We are on a journey of realizing a compassionate civilization community by com-munity, organization by organization, and person by per-son. However, it is only ensured by what you and I and 7.3 billion people do each day. Innovative leadership methods are needed in this effort including group facilitation, social artistry, and integral thinking.

Turn to your neighbor and discuss which of these or other organizations are working in Fairfield or in your commu-nity, what they are doing and where you see collabora-tion of different organizations and movements.

I find that I must take good care of myself so that I can continue the journey of care for all beings everywhere. I am in my 50th year of being a global-local citizen and servant leader and am still passionate about my life of service. Every day, I find ways to cultivate understanding and compassion, realize happiness, celebrate gratitude, live lifelong commit-ment, choose courage again and again, dance with time, and embrace sadness, sickness, old age, and death. I meditate daily, get enough sleep, eat wholesome food, spend time with family, walk in nature, exercise at the gym, read, write, speak, consult, teach, and engage in social and political activism.

How do you take care of yourself for this lifelong jour-ney of care? How do you care for others on the journey? Please share with your neighbor.

Let us continue our journeys of compassionate action for the rest of our lives. Yes! Let us continue to build Fairfield and your town as a Beautiful and Just Meadow of Positive Energy! As a cradle of consciousness! As a citadel of compassion! To show all the communities of Iowa, the USA, and the world what it looks like to realize peace, to achieve the 17 sustainable development goals, to be a multi-cultural society, and much more! Onward! And, do not forget to vote and get out the vote this November 6th, a very, very important election. The next 12 months is phase three of World Fair Field and is all about action in the 17 SDGs. Let's shock the world with sustainable development, so that in September 2019 we have much to celebrate!

Thank you for your participation and wisdom during this interactive keynote, and your full and deep lives of service.

Let's end our interactive keynote by moving into action with our bodies. Please stand up. Let's sway. Let's dance. Hold hands. Raise your arms. Yes, we can!

11

"On Creating a Compassionate Community and World"

Building Creative Communities Conference

Cotton Hall, Colquitt, Georgia, USA
1 February 2019

*F*our months later, the eleventh critical decade call to action, "on creating a compassionate community and world" was heard back in Colquitt, Georgia, USA. I also facilitated a workshop on "discerning your life story." After my keynote, the transformative power of the play-in-a-day led by the Story Bridge team once more demonstrated how to generate community understanding and energy; and the social artistry training equipped community leaders and developers. A video of my talk is on the web.

From Serving People & Planet: "Also in late January and early February, I returned to Colquitt, Georgia, to the Building

Creative Communities Conference and gave a keynote address on creating a compassionate community and civilization and a workshop on discerning your life story. It was wonderful being back in magical Colquitt, the home of Swamp Gravy, especially being with colleagues Joy Jinks, Jan Sanders, and Richard Sims. Again, I experienced the transformative power of the Story Bridge process of a play-in-a-day (PIAD), generating community trust and energy for community development. Dr. Qinghong Wei, executive director of Story Bridge, and Dr. Richard Geer, its founder, proposed partnering with me in future storytelling, planning, and training events based on my book, their process, and my methods of planning and training. I happily agreed." (pages 217 – 218)

Good morning. It is wonderful to be here with you at the beginning of this four-day journey of building creative communities through story, culture, and change. It could be a whole new beginning for each of us. Wasn't Swamp Gravy simply amazing last night? Thank you, Joy Jinks, for inviting me back to Colquitt. I first met Joy when she and her daughter came to Jamaica to volunteer with an ICA community development project that I was leading. I have always been an admirer of her sparkle, intelligence, and zest for life. I have many fond memories from a few years ago of the people, murals, and more while being here with my wife. I must confess that I was worried about all of you in Colquitt during the hurricane. You are grieving. And, you are rebuilding. Blessings. Onward.

Let us see who is here. From Florida/FSU? I am a fan of your Andrew Gillum. Georgia? I am a fan of your Stacey

Abrams. Elsewhere? Furthest? Closest? Youngest? Oldest?

Please relax, breath in and out, focus your gaze downward, and simply be aware of being here and now.

Please turn to a neighbor and share what you hope to achieve by Sunday afternoon.

Let us share a few. Anyone?
This morning, I invite you to think about and discuss an amazing story concerning compassionate action, the crises and opportunities that we face, the principles that can guide us, the areas of transformation where we need to put our energy, and the movement of movements (MOM) that will help us create a compassionate community, America, and world. I will occasionally ask you a question; you will talk and listen to someone near you; and I will share my thoughts. This will be a dialogical story telling keynote, okay?

First, a word about compassion: it is composed of "com" (with) and "passion" (suffering): to be with suffering, another's, and one's own. Compassionate action is not just a feeling; it is not simply empathy. It is decisive action that I or you or someone takes to help relieve the suffering of a living being, someone else, or yourself. I believe that compassionate action is the key to the future of life on Earth.

Now the story.

Once upon a time – now – you and I wake up to the realization that we live in the most critical time in all human history.

Wow! Climate change is threatening human civilization and indeed all life on Earth. The patriarchy is fighting to maintain its control of women, nature, and society. Greed and a rigged economy have increased income and wealth disparities with twenty-six people now having as much wealth as the bottom half of the global population. The rich and their corporations are fighting to control our governments and are weakening democratic institutions to increase their dominance, power, and wealth. Bias and bigotry are in full view and are asserting themselves in the forms of racism, misogyny, religious fundamentalism, homophobia, and genocide. And a culture of violence is pervasive with perpetual warfare and nuclear capability ever present. How are we so fortunate to be alive now?!

Our planet is warming because of the release of carbon dioxide, methane, and other greenhouse gases from the burning of fossil fuels, the raising of animals for meat and other human activities resulting in the melting of ice caps and glaciers, sea rise, coastal flooding, forest fires, mega storms, food collapse, social dislocation, and more. Georgia and Florida have been hit hard. My wife and I have been grieving Panama City where her brother and his family live and have been destabilized. After thousands of years, women are still being subjugated by men resulting in overly masculinized societies based on aggression and cutthroat competition. Billions of people live in poverty because of systems of colonialization, neocolonialization, and globalized capitalism. Wealthy elites and their corporations control our political and economic systems. There is widespread misunderstanding, fear and hatred of people who are of a

different race, ethnicity, religion, culture, or sexual orientation. And, we suffer from armed conflict between and within
nations and ubiquitous violence in everyday life.

These six crises are interdependent and are demanding a
whole system transformation if life on Earth is to continue
and were to thrive.

**How do these crises manifest in your community and
state? Please share with your neighbor.**
Fortunately, we find within selves six deep, human values
and principles that can provide the motivation and direction
needed to confront these crises: sustainability, equality, justice, participation, tolerance, and nonviolence. Sustainability
has to do with longevity, life, and healthy ecosystems. Equality
is a sacred principle that every life is precious and deserves to
exist and to flourish. Justice is a fierce principle of the overcoming of conditions that are unfair or harmful. Participation
is a way of enabling the voice, priorities, and wellbeing of every
person in societal dialogue, policy making, and implementation. Tolerance arises from an understanding that the multitude of unique expressions of being human are each valuable
and have wisdom to share with others. And, nonviolence is a
sacred choice to refrain from doing harm even while holding
firmly to what is right and true. These six principles can carry us
ever forward in our noble quest for a compassionate society.

**Which of these principles or other principles are most
important to you, your life, and your work? Please share
with your neighbor.**

Empowered by these six principles, facing the six crises, we see six areas of transformation that are required of us: environmental sustainability, gender equality, socioeconomic justice, participatory governance, cultural tolerance, and peace and nonviolence.

Environmental sustainability includes the cessation of extracting and burning fossil fuels, protecting biodiversity of other species of animals and plants, protecting the health of water, air, and land, the use of green energy, and mitigating and adapting to climate chaos. Gender equality is the full partnership of women and men with the voices and wisdom of women in leadership positions at all levels of society emphasizing collaboration and caring. Socioeconomic justice includes the provision of quality healthcare, education, and a livable income for all people. Participatory governance is radical, direct democracy in which every person's vote, voice, and priorities are a determining force in the political process. Cultural tolerance includes acceptance and appreciation of differences of religion, ethnicity, race, and culture. And, nonviolence and peace create a world in which armed conflict has lost its legitimacy as a means of dispute resolution in favor of peaceful coexistence and cooperation, and in which nonviolence becomes a way of life. We are grateful that these six areas of transformation are mutually supportive in creating a compassionate community and civilization. For each of these we need to identify and articulate a hoped-for future vision, the obstacles blocking that vision, strategic directions that will overcome the obstacles and move toward the vision, and the action plan and timeline that will achieve the strategies. The ICA's Technology of Participation (ToP) and other methods provide us with the strategic planning process and facilitative methods for planning and implementation. I recall that one of the programs I managed at UNDP was on Decentralizing the MDGs (the precursor of the Sustainable Development Goals [SDGs]) through Innovative Leadership (DMIL) including the use of ToP, integral thinking, and social artistry which you will be experiencing during this conference.

Turn to your neighbor and discuss which of these areas of transformation are being worked on in your community or state or needs to be worked on.

Gratefully there are millions of people of good will, and their organizations, comprising movements that are catalyzing a better world for all. These movements include the environmental movement, the women's movement, the social justice movement, the democracy movement, the human rights movement, and the peace movement. Taken together they make up a massive movement of movements or MOM that is transforming our world for the better. The environmental movement includes organizations such as 350.org, Transition Towns, and Green Peace. Sixteen-year-old Greta Thunberg from Sweden is providing fierce climate leadership. She tells politicians "I don't want your hopes. I want you to deal with the fact that the house is on fire!" The women's movement is made up of many organizations such as NOW and Women for Justice. The social justice movement includes organizations such as labor unions. The democracy movement includes organizations such as Indivisible, Our Revolution, MoveOn, and Democracy Spring. The human rights movement includes organizations such as the ACLU, LGBTQ rights organizations, and Human Rights Watch. And, the peace movement includes many organizations that promote nonviolence, and disarmament, and call for an end to the use of armed conflict. People everywhere are waking up and standing up. We are on a journey of realizing a compassionate civilization community by community, organization by organization, and person by person. However, it is only ensured by what you and I and 7.3 billion people do each day. Innovative leadership methods are needed in this effort including group facilitation, social artistry, and integral thinking.

Turn to your neighbor and discuss which of these or other organizations are working in your community or state, what they are doing and where you see collaboration of different organizations and movements.

I find that I must take good care of myself so that I can continue the journey of care for all beings everywhere. I am in my 50th year of being a global-local citizen and servant leader and am still passionate about my life of service. In my workshop tomorrow, I will share my life story and help you dream your own life story. Every day, I find ways to cultivate understanding and compassion, realize happiness, celebrate gratitude, live lifelong commitment, choose courage again and again, dance with time, and embrace sadness, sickness, old age, and death. I meditate daily, get enough sleep, eat wholesome food, spend time with family, walk in nature, exercise at the gym, read, write, speak, consult, teach, and engage in social and political activism.

How do you take care of yourself for this life-long journey of care? How do you care for others on the journey? Please share with your neighbor.

What would you name this story? Share with your neighbor.

Let us continue our journeys of compassionate action for the rest of our lives. Yes! Let us continue to build Colquitt, and other communities as compassionate, just, and sustainable to show all the communities of Georgia, Florida, the USA, and the world what it looks like. Onward! And, do not forget to vote and get out the vote in 2020, an especially important election. Let us shock the world with sustainable, compassionate development so that we have much to celebrate!

Thank you for your participation and wisdom during this interactive keynote, and for your full and deep lives of service. This keynote is based on my book *A Compassionate Civilization: The Urgency of Sustainable Development and Mindful Activism.*

Let us end our interactive keynote by moving into action with our bodies. Please stand up. Let's sway. Let's dance. Hold hands. Raise your arms. Yes, we can!

12

"The Archives, The Movement of Movements, and a Utopic Vision"

Presentation for the ICA Social Research Center Sojourn

GreenRise, Chicago, Illinois, USA
16 April 2019

*T*he twelfth and final critical decade call to action was presented back in Chicago at the headquarters of ICA USA where I began the journey of talks in 2010. This time it was given at the ICA Social Research Center archives sojourn. A video of the talk is on Facebook. My challenge to the colleagues was to share ICA's sixty years of effective social, educational, and spirit methods and models with the movement of movements (MoM) for the sake of creating a compassionate community,

151

nation, and world. The full ICA archives can be found on the web (see bibliography).

From Serving People & Planet: *"In April, I participated once more in the ICA archives sojourn in Chicago, including giving a presentation on how the archives can be injected into the movement of movements. Colleagues Herman Greene, Nelson Stover, and Olive Ann Slotta also made early morning presentations. At the Archives meeting, the ICA Ukraine representative, Svitlana Salamatova, announced that her organization would prepare a Ukrainian language edition of my book. When it was ready, they want me to go to Ukraine to meet and speak with supporters of this cause. Other national ICAs were considering Hindi-, Chinese-, Spanish-, and Arabic-language editions. We also celebrated the completed life of our dear colleague Jean Long, the Archives Project coordinator. A surprise happened in the basement of the ICA GreenRise. While I was being shown around by colleague Ruth Gilbert, I reached into a random storage box and pulled out a book, opened it, and saw my mother's handwritten note inside, giving this gift to Mary and me for our first Christmas together in 1968." (page 219)*

Dr. Tatwa Timsina the founder of ICA Nepal, had my book, *A Compassionate Civilization*, translated into Nepali and printed, and gave a copy to every member of parliament, every provincial minister, and every cabinet minister in hopes that it would spark a dialogue about the future of Nepal as a compassionate society. That is his vision. I was amazed and honored. They are following up with discussion groups in the parliament. One ICA Nepal colleague is a member of parliament and is leading the study. There is a lot of

ICA in the book. I do not know if you have read it, but there are a lot of ICA methods and ICA wisdom, and other wisdom in the book. We did not have all the wisdom, right, maybe only 98% (laughter.) There was some left over for some other groups. It kept us humble. Thank you, Tatwa, for what you are doing in your country. We are all doing what we can.

Our colleague, the late Jean Long, is also helping give this presentation. She was interested in the movement of movements. I want to honor her memory, and we will do that throughout this week. I brought a book of poetry to read at the memorial dinner; I am sure you did also. She was a powerful presence. When someone is a powerful presence, they are a powerful absence when they are absent. We have that as our reality.

I do not want to start with the movement of movements. I want to start with the ICA archives. Can you tell what this chart is? The archives include structural reformulation, con- textual re-education, and spirit re-motivation. How do we share sixty years of knowledge, methods, experience, and wisdom? It is kind of like our collective autobiography. I am working on my autobiography, and it is not easy. There is so much to remember, and interpret, and decide if it is share- able, worth sharing. Can it enable others and be helpful? My wife said on the way to the airport: the archives are also like a presidential library. When she visited Jimmie Carter's presidential library, she was so impressed and touched by the wisdom there. So, whether it is the real stuff, the paper, or the online stuff, which of course is also real, it is a gift. It is our gift, the gift that keeps on giving. We in this room are the living archives, as well as colleagues all over the world. And of course, we also need the paper, and the website. How can these methods and wisdom help equip the movement of movements and inform its strategies, deal with the blocks facing humanity, and help realize a hoped-for-vision of the future?

There are two futures possible. We do not know what will happen. Have you heard of Greta Thunberg of Sweden? She is a fifteen-year-old, on the autism spectrum, an incredible global leader of the climate movement. Every Friday, she would sit outside the Swedish parliament and protest with Friday School Strike for Climate. Now, 1.5 million children in 128 countries are doing it, because of Greta. She says that autism is a gift; it allows her to focus like a laser. When you have autism, you can really focus. Those of us who do not have it are so monkey minded. We are jumping all over the place. But with autism, you can focus like a laser beam. And, she is focusing. She says, I do not want you to have hope. I want you to panic. The house is on fire. I do not want you to have hope, and thoughts, and prayers.

It is a time for action, for activism. The house is on fire, folks, you know that. I could quote a lot of statistics but will not. So, one possible future is dystopia. We are in ecocide. We are killing off plants and animals, polluting our soils, air, and water at horrendous rates. Again, I will not give you the statistics. We are committing ecocide and "species-cide". We are killing life on Earth. We did not know we were going to do it. We thought we were making progress. We thought, oil is good. It is creating energy. And, we thought the consumption-production economy was good. It is producing jobs and wealth. So, we are doing a lot of things that we thought were good but had unintended consequences.

Now, we know about these consequences; and it is time to make radical change. Greta says, we need a whole new way of thinking. We need a whole new paradigm, mindset, worldview. We cannot continue as we are. If we do, we are headed toward a dystopic future. Now, that is not where I am putting my mind. I want us to move toward utopia. Has anyone read the little book, *Utopia for Realists*? It is written by a Dutchman, Rutger Bregman, who recently confronted the World Economic Forum. He said, you guys, forget your philanthropy. You need to be giving ninety percent of your income to taxes. And they were furious with him. They hate him. Have a look at it, a wonderful little book. Among other things, he writes about universal basic income – UBI – that every human being by virtue of being alive should have a way of living, because we are human beings. One approach is that everyone should receive one thousand dollars a month. Now that is not a lot, but it provides a kind of foundation or floor.

A utopic future is one in which people and planet are in harmony, and people and people are in harmony. It is possible. Now, utopia is not utopian. It is a vision, a hope, a dream; and we are the people of the dream. We ICA folk, we facilitators, ask questions over and over: what is your dream of a hoped-for future? What are your hopes and dreams for the future, whether it is five years, ten years, or one hundred years? So, which will it be? Will we head toward utopia or dystopia? It depends on what you and I do, and 7.3 billion people around the planet who are involved in this effort. Yet, it is not a time simply to hope. It is a time to panic and act – to change our laws, change our mindsets, change our systems – a whole system transformation. So, how are our ICA archived methods and sixty years of experience and wisdom going to help move humanity toward a utopic future, rather than dystopia?

We must share our methods and experience with the movement of movements (MoM). This includes the environmental movement – climate change mitigation and adaptation, green energy, protecting ecosystems, and so on; the women's movement – bringing the full participation of the wisdom and knowledge of half of humanity which has heretofore been subjugated; although it has changed a lot in recent years. However, it is shocking to realize how recently women have been voting in the US – only ninety years! And there are some people who do not want this to continue. There are also the social justice movement, the democracy movement – getting everyone's voice into political decision making, the human rights movement – every human being has the right to exist and flourish, and the peace movement.

When these movements begin to cooperate, they form a MoM, a movement of movements, because they are no longer merely separate movements. They are now each embodying the other. Have you heard of Rev. Dr. Barber in North Carolina, the founder of the Poor Peoples' Campaign, an incredible effort following up the work of Rev. Dr. Martin Luther King Jr? I intend to get involved in that. I hope you will consider that also. The Poor Peoples' Movement is concerned with social justice, climate justice, racial justice, and democratic participation. So, that is an example of one effort that is bringing these themes together. And, the Fridays for School Strike for the Climate is also concerned with ecology, justice, equity, and participation. The movement of movements is the collaboration of these six movements, and many more movements. I have identified six for the sake of simplicity. There are hundreds of movements, including the organic food movement, the LGBTQ movement, and many more, that are driving us toward a more human future. There are also movements that are not, but I will not go into that.

How do we get our ICA and other methods and wisdom into the movement of movements? Some of the ways include through the archives' website, and training and planning events. Do you remember our early model of movement building? It includes interchange, training, research, and demonstration.

We called this the global movement of "those who care" (TWC), or the spirit movement. Karen Armstrong, the founder of Charter of Compassion International, calls it the network of networks. Paul Hawken calls it the Big Movement. Herman Hesse calls it the League. Kazantzakis calls it the Crimson Line. There is a force moving humanity toward a more human future throughout history that we are part of.

What is blocking humanity from moving toward a possible future of utopia that we want to realize if possible, and away from a dystopic future that we want to avoid if possible?

What are the blocks? The blocks include climate chaos and ecocide, and patriarchy and misogyny. Did you know that there are states right now in this country which are trying to put the death penalty on women who have an abortion after six weeks? Can you believe it?! This is outrageous. This manifests a dystopic future. Another block is systemic poverty. Poverty is not an accident, folks. Society has been designed to create a sliver of rich people, lots of poor people, and a few middleclass people. By design, most of the wealth in the last several years has gone to the .01 percent of the population. Wealth used to go to the emperor and the nobility, and now goes to the billionaires, the hedge fund managers, and the CEOs. Another block is fascist plutocracy. What is that? Plutocracy is the rule of the rich. Fascism is based on "might makes right", that gaining and maintaining power and wealth is all that matters, not the wellbeing of citizens and nature. Right now, in this country we have a government that is a fascist plutocracy. And, it is spreading around the world, including Brazil, and wherever there are "strong men" controlling the society – Turkey, North Korea, and others. This is driving us toward a dystopic future.

Another block is racism and bigotry. After all this time, there are some who are saying, you are different, and I hate you. This is xenophobia, a fear of the other, other races, religions, and sexual orientations. Another block to a hoped-for future is perpetual war and a culture of violence. This country has spent six trillion dollars on wars since 9/11 and killed 500,000 people. For what? This fortune could have gone toward so much that is good. I call it a "culture" of violence because we assume, we presuppose, we believe that violence is okay and necessary. We have armies that kill people. We have police that shoot people if they look different. These crises, blocks, and contradictions are driving us toward a dystopic future. How do we rather move toward a utopic future of harmony of people with people and nature, heaven on Earth, the Beloved Community?

So, how can the sixty years of methods, models, and wisdom of the EI/ICA archives be shared with and equip the movement of movements?

There are six strategies for the movement of movements to deal with the blocks, crises, and contradictions, and move toward a utopic future. These include, first, creating environmental sustainability and regenerative development. Planet Earth is not simply a set of resources for humans to use up. It is a living ecosystem that sustains all life; it is Gaia, the Earth goddess. The Earth is alive. We need to revisit our ideology, that all the Earth and all the resources belong to all the people. No, rather, we humans belong to, are part of, the Earth. The Earth is breathing in and out, moving with her air, water, soil, plants, animals, and humans, giving birth to ever new species.

The second strategy is promoting gender equality. Ed Feldmanis and I have good discussions about this on Facebook. Yes, men are also equal. But since women have been put down for thousands of years, it is a little helpful to emphasize women's empowerment and equality. Yes, Ed, men have been forgotten or seen as the enemy in many parts of the world. Yes, I agree that we must not forget that men can be good too. (laughter) We men must be as good as we can be; we have a lot of work to do on ourselves and our ideas about ourselves and about women and about our behavior.

The third strategy is socio-economic justice. We need UBI, universal basic income. Naomi Klein is so clear that unbridled capitalism is killing the Earth and humanity. Flying back to North Carolina may be my last flight. Greta says that we must stop eating meat and flying, because of their negative climate impacts; and we should drive an electric or hybrid vehicle or ride a bicycle. Greta takes only trains; she took a sailboat across the Atlantic; she will not fly; her parents will not fly. Her mother is an opera singer and her father an actor. May the Greta's of this world lead us into a new future.

The fourth strategy is participatory governance, that everyone has a voice, not just the wealthy and powerful, in how we organize ourselves as human beings. The fifth strategy is cultural tolerance, to allow someone else to be different from you. Then maybe someday, we can grow to understand why a person is the way they are. First, let us just give each other the right to exist. The sixth strategy is to promote nonviolence and peace.

We need to drive our wisdom into the movement of move-ments to realize the six strategies that break through the roadblocks and move us toward a utopic future. However, there is no certainty. I am sorry to tell you. If you say that you know that this will all be successful, then you have given up. You are no longer on the front line. It is confusing is it not? We must have a dream of a hoped-for future, yet we must not rely on hope and certainty. We should panic and drive forward with action. This is our moment. That is it.

How do we get our and other wisdom into the movement of movements? In my view, ICA's Technology of Participation (ToP) should be the default method in governance processes at every level. ToP trained leaders should be helping facilitate governance discussions at every level – community, town, city, county, state, nation, and global. We have many colleagues around the world who are giving their lives to promote the use of or training in ToP methods and processes. Tatwa asked if he could change the subtitle of my book in the Nepali edition. I said sure. And, they get 100% of sales proceeds. I am sure they will make millions. (laughter) The subtitle in the Nepali edition is not the Urgency of Sustainable Development and Mindful Activism. It is Effective Leadership Methods. This is because Tatwa wants to drive ToP and social artistry into the parliament and other governmental forums in Nepal.

So, we share our methods with the MoM which uses them to actualize the strategies to breakthrough the blocks and move toward a hoped-for future. Okay, let us discuss.

Epilogue
Reflections on the Critical
Decade 2020 – 2029

What do you remember from these talks? What were some of the feelings and thoughts you had as you encountered them? For you, what is the significance of these talks and ideas? What will you do in the days ahead because you have read them? Please take some time to reflect on those questions. You might choose to write down your thoughts, or you might want to discuss with someone.

What was the impact of these talks on the critical decade of 2010 – 2019 you might ask? I find that cause and effect are exceedingly difficult if not impossible to identify with most things in life. Giving the talks certainly impacted me. I felt that I was spreading an urgent message far and wide, calling people to wake up and take action to avoid doing greater harm and to move toward a better world for all. The talks did not slow down or stop climate chaos or any of the other crises. The talks did not bring about a new civilization of compassion. Why do we do what we do when we cannot know our impact? This is true of so much in life: parenting, teaching, speaking, writing, acting. We do what we decide we must do, what we are called to do. And, we must leave the judgment concerning impact to history.

Well, the previous critical decade came and went, and we entered the "real" or *final* or at least the current critical decade. We are now in the early days of a global COVID-19 pandemic that is deadly, disabling, highly contagious, and socially and economically disruptive. Responsible leadership and mass compliance have been shown to be key factors in whether a country has been able to stop the pandemic or not. Climate fires have engulfed the US west coast. Authoritarian plutocracy is saying a firm no to fair elections and charging ahead with its agenda of transferring trillions of dollars to the 1%. People are committed to voting with their votes counted, or else democracy may come to an end. Racism is seen as systemic and police violence is on the rise as well as the Black Lives Matter movement.

Women's rights are more in danger than ever, even as women have been shown to be the most effective national leaders in managing and stopping the pandemic as in Germany, New Zealand, Taiwan, and elsewhere. Much of the economy of Main Street has collapsed as businesses have shut down and gone bankrupt. Millions of people have lost their income and may lose their homes. Wall Street is booming with billionaires and millionaires making a windfall.

Artificial Intelligence (AI) may be threatening jobs, income, and survival. Truth, facts, and decency have suffered under a constant barrage of falsehood, distraction, and personal attacks. People are traumatized by unremitting chaos and a continuous series of scandals.

The viral pandemic is linked to several other pandemics battering us, to name just a few, the systemic racism pandemic, the ecocide/climate pandemic, the wealth-hoarding/ systemic poverty pandemic, the misogyny/patriarchy pandemic, the violence/warfare pandemic, and the fascism/plutocracy pandemic. I have been writing and speaking about these six pandemics for the past ten years or so, but the viral pandemic was so sudden, confusing and distracting, that my brain and heart could not relate it to these other six, when actually, it is not separate from them.

Two words came to me: mortality and morality. The viral pandemic shocked me/us into facing that today, not in ten years, I could die, which is related to, someday I will most certainly die: mortality. Many people had already been talking about the death of ecosystems and the likely death of human civilization, but suddenly, almost the whole human race woke up to the fact that our species was under attack and my body and ego were threatened at this very moment. Yes, climate chaos of floods, fires, super storms, and food shortages may wipe us out, and we were already being assaulted by the other five pandemics, but in an instant, we were in mortal danger. And, my loved ones and I are on thin ice.

Awareness of our own mortality can make us more awake and sensitive. We can become more reflective, and grateful, or we can become traumatized and fearful, or some of both. It is in this state of being, that we may be more open to responding to other people's suffering and may try to relieve that suffering – thus the protests over the tragic death of George Floyd, and so many others, as well as the systemic features of racism.

Now, morality: we humans are arguing and fighting about what is true or false and what is right or wrong. Are black and brown people actually equal to white people or are they even people at all? Is climate chaos really happening or is it a hoax? Is it right that a few billionaires have more wealth than half of humanity? Do women have the same importance and rights as men? If you fear or hate someone is it okay or even necessary to kill them? And, isn't democracy a crazy notion which should be replaced once and for all by strongman rule (yes, *man*), representing a superior race and religion, and being one of the rich who have well demonstrated their superiority? Aren't those other people not even worthy of life, liberty and the pursuit of happiness: the disgusting black and brown people, the weak-minded women, the immoral gays and trans, the pansy liberals, and the poor who are obviously losers? The belief in one's superiority can lead to some of the greatest evils of humankind.

Or is it true that all people are of infinite value and that society is indeed obligated to enable each person to realize her or his full potential in this life? Should we not be doing everything we can to mitigate and adapt to climate chaos to protect life on Earth? Is it not necessary to distribute wealth through taxation and universal basic income (UBI) to care for everyone? Doesn't everyone deserve health-care? Are women not half of humanity with unique wisdom and gifts of leadership that society desperately needs? Is democracy not required to ensure that every voice counts, that every person can help govern human society? Isn't war depraved and shouldn't it be abolished as an option for con-flict resolution?

These are all questions of morality. What is right and good for human beings to embody and act out on this Earth?

Now comes the virus of death. The recognition of a COVID-19 pandemic woke up many people concerning who gets to live and who gets to die. The people most likely to die of the virus are the poor – mostly black and brown peo-ple, the sick, the elderly (those already approaching death), and "essential" workers many of whom are wage-slaves and/ or saints. But these are many of the same people whose lives are already being cut short by climate chaos, poverty, misogyny, racism, fascism, and war. There is so much unnec-essary cruelty and suffering. Many of us find ourselves often in tears or outrage.

What is true? What is right and good behavior? The wisdom traditions and historical religions all advocate acts of love, compassion, kindness, justice, and forgiveness. But much of modern culture promotes cutthroat competition, domination, ego, self-interest and pleasure, greed, bias, fear, and violence. Scientists are increasingly showing, however, that our basic

nature is indeed one of mutual concern, care, and cooperation. And in any case, since our lives are so noticeably short,
can't we simply be kind to one another?

How are we humans going to facilitate this societal dialogue and this transformation? How are we going to care for
people and planet? Personally, I am not sure of the answer.
What are your thoughts? What would you propose?

After fifty years of trying to catalyze a better world, I am
perplexed.

One thing I do know, however, is that we must not give up.
We must each do everything we can to manifest our care for
family and friends, the weak and the vulnerable, both near at
hand and far away, and the ecosystems of plants, animals, air,
water, and soil. We are one human family. We are one Earth
family. We must get out the vote, speak, and write what is
true and loving, facilitate dialogue, act responsibly, care for
those in need, and engage in nonviolent direct action. We *can*
catalyze a compassionate-ecological civilization, community
by community, organization by organization, and network
by network. In fact, there is already a movement of movements (MoM) at work around the world doing just that. And
the speed at which the whole world responded to the virus is
proof that we can change quickly to crisis.

After being a community developer, policy advisor, facilitator, professor, and consultant, I am now focusing on being
an ecosystem/justice activist, and a nonfiction author. I will
keep writing, speaking out, and demonstrating care for others. What about you?

May the critical decade of 2020 – 2029 be a time of healing and transformation, a turning away from dystopia to

embrace a "utopia for realists" as Rutger Bregman put it in his book by the same name. And, may we meet the inevitable suffering of the many pandemics with compassion for ourselves and others. For life is fleeting but is very, very good.

Acknowledgments

Gratitude and appreciation:

To those who invited me to give these talks and keynotes, and/or wrote pre-publication reviews of this book, including Adriana Alberti, PhD, of UNDESA; Terry Bergdall, PhD, of ICA USA; Joy Jinks, of the Building Creative Communities Conference; Karen Johnson, of Horace Mann School; Richard Beall, PhD, and Kaye Jacob, of the Maharishi School; Tatwa Timsina, PhD, and Ishu Subba, of ICA Nepal; Rev. Dr. Mark Davies, of Oklahoma City University; Lynda Cock and the late Jean Long, of the ICA Social Research Center Archives project; John Burbidge, of ICA Seattle; Mary Kurian D'Souza of ICA India; and Jo Nelson of ICA Associates (Canada).

To the fine people from around the world who heard, dialogued with, and acted on the ideas in my talks and keynotes given in Bahrain, Nepal, Republic of Korea, Tanzania, India, Chicago, Seattle, Colquitt (Georgia,) New York City, Fairfield, (Iowa,) and Oklahoma City.

To colleagues for their advice before, and feedback after these talks were given, including Jan Sanders, Qinghong

Wei, PhD, Richard Geer, PhD, Svitlana Salamatova, Richard Beall, PhD, Matthew Lindberg-Work, and Jack Gillis.

To friends for sharing their views on social media during the preparation of this book, including Janet Sanders, Debra-Harris-Watson, Isobel Bishop, Chic Dambach, Marti Nicholson, Jan Loubser, Ronnie Seagren, Sabita Koirala Paudyal, Jawad S. Haddadin, Nancy Trask, Elsa Bengel, Dawn Collins, Kevin Jones, Kushendra Mahat, Judi White, Ali Weller, Larry Ward, Puthrika Moonesinghe, Richard David Hames, David Elliott, Kay Schnizlein, Pat Webb, Courtney Bruch, Christina Welty, Jo Nelson, Adriana Alberti, Bruce Schuman, Wanda Holcombe, Jonathan Dudding, Mary Ann Bennett Rosberg, Christiane Meunier, Sophie Donde, Kerry Christopher Dugan, Ricardo Oliveira Neves, Terry Bergdall, Brian Griffith, Wayne Marshall Jones, Arnold Karen, A. M. Noel, Saundra Gerrell Kelley, John B. Hoag, and Judy Fishel.

To Ronnie Seagren for two hours of helpful questions and advice.

To my wise wife, Bonnie Myotai Treace, for her insightful suggestions and loving support.

Appendix One
Author's Videos, Podcasts, Websites, and Books

Author's Online Resources:

Videos of author's speeches:
Chicago. ICA USA International Dev. Think Tank Keynote. 2010: https://www.youtube.com/user/bergdall2

Seoul. UN Forum Workshop Presentation. 2014: https://www.youtube.com/watch?v=KQ3E1AZqFgw

Oklahoma City. OCU Peace Symposium Keynote. 2014: https://vimeo.com/89274462

Fairfield, Iowa. World's Fairfield Peace Symposium Keynote. 2018: https://www.youtube.com/watch?v=hSI5cHwS4TY& featur e=youtu.be

Colquitt, Georgia. Building Creative Communities Conference Keynote. 2019: https://www.youtube.com/channel/UCf6RH m5Hy-KT63DDsb9Ymlg/

Chicago. ICA USA Archives Collegium Presentation. 2019: https://www.facebook.com/icaukraine/videos/ 283358729261479/zpfSTEzNzI4NDg1NjU6MTAyMTg3 Mzc1MzM0NTQxMTM/

Podcasts of radio interviews with author:

North Carolina. *Thinking of Travel*. 2017: http://speakingof-travel.net.buzzsprout.com/18461/603428-robertson-work-shares-how-to-become-a-global-local-citizen

Arizona. *Democratic Perspectives* #1. 2018: http://verde-valleyindependentdemocrats.org/2018/01/17/creating-more-compassionate-communities/

Arizona. *Democratic Perspectives* #2. 2018: http://verde-valleyindependentdemocrats.org/2018/04/03/robertson-work-interview-podcast-april-2-2018/

Websites with author's interview, article, or book excerpt:

Buddhadoor website author interview. 2018: https://www.buddhistdoor.net/features/creating-a-compassionate-civilization-an-interview-with-robertson-work

Garrison Institute website excerpt of ACC. 2017: https://www.garrisoninstitute.org/blog/catalyzing-empathic-engaged-citizens/

ICA International website excerpt of ACC. 2017: http://www.ica-international.org/2017/08/14/compassionate-civilization-urgency-sustainable-development-mindful-activism-reflections-recommendations-rob-work/

American Buddhist Perspectives website excerpt of ACC. 2018: https://www.patheos.com/blogs/americanbuddhist/2018/02/burn-never-guide-compassionate-mindful-activism.html

Progressive Buddhism website excerpt of ACC. 2018: https://progressivebuddhism.blogspot.com/2018/02/how-can-we-build-coalitions-in-this.html

NYU Wagner website article on ACC. 2017: https://wagner.nyu.edu/news/story/prof-robertson-work-out-book-compassionate-civilization-urgency-sustainable-development

Author's Social Media Sites:

A Compassionate Civilization (ACC):
Amazon: https://www.amazon.com/dp/1546972617

Blogsite: https://compassionatecivilization.blogspot.com/

Facebook   page: https://www.facebook.com/
compassionatecivilization/

Movement of Movements (MOM) Facebook page: https://
www.facebook.com/movementofmovementsMOM/

Robertson Work:

Facebook page: https://www.facebook.com/robertson.work

LinkedIn   page: https://www.linkedin.com/in/robertson-
work/Twitter page: https://twitter.com/robertsonwork

Amazon author's page: https://www.amazon.com/Robertson-
Work/e/B075612GBF%3Fref=dbs_a_mng_rwt_scns_share

Author's website: https://www.robertsonwork.com/

Author's Publications:
Work, Robertson. 2020. *Earthling Love: Living Poems*.
Swannanoa NC: Compassionate Civilization Press.

_____. 2020. *Serving People & Planet: In Mystery,
Love, and Gratitude*. Swannanoa NC: Lulu Press.

_____. 2017. *A Compassionate Civilization: The Urgency of Sustainable Development and Mindful Activism – Reflections and Recommendations.* Swannanoa NC: Compassionate Civilization Collaborative (C3).

_____. 2010. "Civil Society Innovations in Governance Leadership: International Demonstrations of Integral Development, the Technology of Participation (ToP), and Social Artistry". pages 112 – 130. *Engaging Civil Society: Emerging Trends in Democratic Governance.* editors Cheema, G. Shabbir, and Popovski, Vesselin. Tokyo: UN University Press.

_____. 2001. "Decentralization, Governance, and Sustainable Regional Development". pages 21 – 34. *New Regional Development Paradigms, Vol. 3, Decentralization, Governance, and the New Planning for Local-Level Development.* editors, Stohr, Walter B., et al. Westport CT: Greenwood Press.

_____. 2003. "Decentralizing Governance: Participation and Partnership in Service Delivery to the Poor". pages 195 – 218. *Reinventing Government for the Twenty-First Center: State Capacity in a Globalizing Society.* Editors. Rondinelli, Dennis A., and Cheema, G. Shabbir. Bloomfield CT: Kumarian Press.

_____. 2003. "Overview of Decentralization Worldwide: A Steppingstone to Improved Governance and

Human Development". pages 3 – 24. *Decentralization & Power Shift: An Imperative for Good Governance – A Sourcebook on Decentralization and Federalism Experiences, Vol. 11: Federalism: The Future of Decentralizing States.* Editors. Brillantes, Jr., Alex B, et al. Manila: Asian Resource Center for Decentralization/UNDP Philippines.

_____. Editor. 1997. *Participatory Local Governance: LIFE's Method and Experience 1992 – 1997.* New York: UNDP.

_____. Editor. 2005. *Pro-Poor Urban Governance: Lessons from LIFE 1992 – 2005.* New York: UNDP.

_____. 1998. "The Role of Development Assistance in the Area of Decentralization". pages 51 – 56. *International Symposium on Local Development and the Role of Government: New Perspectives on Development Assistance.* JICA. Tokyo: IIC/JICA

_____. 1995. "LIFE". pages 90 – 91. *Public Sector Management, Governance, and Sustainable Human Development.* MDGD/BPPS/UNDP. New York: UNDP.

_____. 2007. "The Global Citizen: A Love Story," pages 50 – 56, *Life Lessons for Loving the Way You Live: 7 Essential Ingredients for Finding Balance and Serenity.* Hawthorne, Jennifer Read. Deerfield Beach FL: Health Communications.

_____. 2009. "Strengthening Governance and Public Administration Capacities for Development: A UN ECOSOC Background Paper." New York: UN.

_____. 1993, *LIFE Mission Reports: Jamaica, Brazil, Pakistan, Thailand, Senegal, Tanzania, Egypt, Morocco.* New York: UNDP.

_____. 1994. *LIFE Report on the Global Advisory Committee and Donor Workshop, Stockholm: First Year Review and Strategic Planning.* New York: UNDP.

_____. 1995. *LIFE Report of the Second Annual Global Advisory Committee Workshop, Cairo: Phase 1 Assessment and Phase 2 Strategies.* New York: UNDP.

Appendix Two
Two Talks Given Before the Critical Decade

*A*s a "bonus," two talks given before the critical decade of 2010 – 2019 are included below. These provide a context of the UN's work of sustainable human development, and ICA's role in relation to that.

A.
ICAI Global Conference on Human Development
Lonavala, India, 1994

B.
ICA Dialogue on Urban Human Development
Seattle, Washington, USA, 1995

A.

"Sustainable Human Development: A Process of Participatory Partnerships for Social Equity and Ecological Harmony"

ICA International Annual Global Human Development Conference

Lonavala, India,
4 October 1994

After being a UNDP policy advisor for four years, I was invited to speak at a global conference of ICA International held in India. Since this coincided with my official mission to India, I happily agreed. In the talk, I shared some of things I was learn-ing in the UN system about international development about which I thought my ICA colleagues would be interested. I also spoke about the important work of ICA International and men-tioned several staff who had already helped me in my work at UNDP.

Introduction

My dear colleagues, this is a special opportunity to be together this week in Lonavala, in spite of the plague, at a global gathering of persons associated with the Institute of Cultural Affairs in order to dialogue concerning "Culture in the Transformation Process". This is a time to share (the reports yesterday where impressive and encouraging), a time to reflect, a time to change ones perceptions, a time to design the future, a time to celebrate, and a time to recom-mit oneself to facilitating the whole system transition that is happening on planet Earth.

This transition, which is taking place at a dazzling speed, involves profound changes in the mental constructs with which we "create the world". For example, a major para-digm shift took place, a few weeks ago in Cairo at the UN Conference on Population and Development. Before this meeting, people thought in terms of a "population crisis" and the need for "birth control" requiring interventionist strategies and resulting in a divisive debate about how births were or were not to be controlled and by whom. After the Cairo event, we are thinking about how to empower women, through education, jobs, credit, political voice, and health, to make choices about what happens to their bodies and their lives. We have decided to think about the impact of development, not control, on population. This is a shift from a crisis/control model to an opportunity/empowerment model, from a hardware approach to a software approach. Another major paradigm shift took place in Rio two years ago at the Earth Summit, but I want to come back to this later.

Since April, when Mary D'Souza invited me to participate and make a presentation related to building partnerships for sustainable development, I have been thinking about this meeting. During that time, I have reflected on the twenty-seven years that I have been engaged in international development, immediately following graduate school, in villages, slums, and board rooms around the world, first as a staff member of a nongovernmental organization (NGO) network, called the Order Ecumenical/ Ecumenical Institute/Institute of Cultural Affairs (OE/EI/ ICA), for which I am profoundly grateful.

Four years ago, a few days after I had been asked to work with the United Nations Development Programme, (UNDP), Mary, my wife, and I took a tour of UN headquarters in New York City. Near the display on disarmament, we came upon a new exhibit about the role of NGOs that was just being painted on the wall. As we searched the list, we were excited to see on the wall of the UN, along with the other NGOs with the UN Economic and Social Council (ECOSOC) consultative status, the name "Institute of Cultural Affairs International." Suddenly everything came together, and we reflected that many of us had the UN, and what it could mean for our planet, in our minds and in our daily prayers for many years.

Today I want to speak to you, to think with you, about international development, as an international civil servant, as a staff member of UNDP. UNDP is the central coordinating and funding body of the UN family of agencies and has offices in 131 developing countries. My work is with the Urban Development Unit within the Management Development and Governance Division at UNDP Headquarters and deals with coordinating the Local Initiative Facility for Urban Environment the LIFE Program.

ICA International (ICAI) is an important global network of NGOs and private consultants which has collaborated with UNDP in many ways over the years including the International Exposition of Rural Development (IERD) which brought many of us to India 10 years ago. UNDP felt that this meeting in Lonavala was important enough to send a representative. And, I thought that the themes of this event were intriguing enough to request that I be that representative. My wife Mary had hoped to be here, but her master's degree studies, and family counseling schedule were too demanding at this time of year.

I. What is development? What is humanness?
In 1986, Dr. Joep van Arendonk of the UN Fund for Population Activities (UNFPA), a sister organization of UNDP, raised two profound questions at the ICA global meeting in Bilbao, Spain. He asked, "What is development?" and "What is humanness?" These two questions, coming from a UN

official, stopped my world and captured my imagination. Joep said that asking people these questions, not providing answers, is what the world needs. Each country, each community, each person needs to answer these questions. The challenge is to catalyze a societal dialogue which allows everyone's answer to be heard and honored in an integrated fashion. He also said that these questions must be related to tangible efforts to improve people's lives such as a new water pump in a village.

In raising the question, what is development, let us step back and take a quick sweep through the "development" of our species – the evolution of a species on our planet. Science places our emergence some 2 million years ago, making us newcomers on a planet that is 4 billion years old and in a universe that has been evolving for some 13 billion years. Through trial and error, we developed dexterity, tool making, speech, community, agriculture, ritual, and music. We developed towns, religions, cultures, history, cities, and empires. We developed trade, politics, and currencies. We developed nation-states, industrialization, colonialism, science, atomic bombs, televisions, spaceships, and computers. And, our evolution continues.

We entered the 20th Century full of the belief in the inevitability of progress. It took two world wars and a global depression to shatter this expectation. After the second world war, the victors set about developing the vanquished. The United Nations was born with the declaration that "We the people" must put aside the option of war and seek peace and development. During the Cold War, international agencies, both governmental and non-governmental, including the ICA, were created to bring development to the "undeveloped", the "underdeveloped" and the "developing". (What a grand mission!) We have seen great gains in longevity, in literacy, in basic services delivery, in economic development which included the emergence of the Asian tigers, in trade, science, and technology. In the 1980s, we experienced the lost decade of development with some nations particularly in Africa sliding back into the bush. And now in the post-Cold War era, we are raising the question anew, what is international development cooperation? And in the 1990s, we are assaulted by the HIV/AIDS epidemic, jobless economic growth, the degradation of the environment, civil wars, ethnic hatred, massive migration, the collapse of the family, donor fatigue, and growing poverty. Poverty, disease, and violence carry no passports. When the North becomes aware of this fact, its inextricable link to the South is clearly exposed.

In summary, we are experiencing both breakdown and break through, or what Jean Houston calls "whole system transition".

And as for the question of "What is humanness?", what is it that is developing, evolving, unfolding? What is the essential nature of our species? Are we, first and foremost, economic animals of production and consumption? Are we driven by the desire for power, sex, and greed? Are we controlled by our fears and angst? Must we be controlled by a hierarchy of authority lest we spin out of control? Or are we spiritual beings? Are we "the universe become conscious of itself."?

Are we made in the image of God? Are we love incarnate? Or are we all of this and much, much more? Our answer to this second question is critical to our understanding of what is indeed developing and how we go about "development". For me, an anthropology of the "consciousness of consciousness of consciousness" is the most all embracing and profound; but again, every individual, community, and nation must answer this question as manifested in daily existence.

II. Sustainable Human Development (SHD): A New Paradigm of International Development Cooperation

At the beginning of this decade, UNDP began publishing the annual "Human Development Report" (HDR). This independent analysis raised the question of human development and began to shift the debate within the development establishment from a singular focus on macro economic indicators, such as Gross National Product (GNP), which the World Bank and others had promoted, to a range of social and economic indicators, including longevity, literacy, and adjusted GNP per capita. The HDR suggested that the question which must be raised is "how are the people faring?" not "what is a nation's gross national product per capita". Wide disparities were noticed between GNP and real living conditions of the people. Some nations, such as Sri Lanka, with a lower GNP per capita than say Brazil, had a higher Human Development Index (HDI) – a composite of longevity, literacy, and GNP per capita adjusted for distribution and purchasing power. The HDR suggested that human development had to do with increasing the capacity of people to make choices about their lives. Many groups, including the ICA, had two decades previously made this shift to human development, but it was now entering the mainstream.

Then in May 1992, the UN Earth Summit took place. This event was a global wake up call to sustainable development. We saw that the planet was imperiled. After centuries of unrestricted industrial growth with its accompanying pollution and environmental degradation, and the persistent and massive poverty of the human family, our common sense began to shift. If human beings do not care for the water, the soil, the air, the forests, and the diverse species of planet Earth, including our own, then we and indeed all living beings are at risk. People began to see the Earth as a whole system and even as a living organism.

A new paradigm of development was being born on the global stage. As stated in the July 1992 high-level meeting of the UN's ECOSOC, there is an "emerging vision of development as human-centered, equitable, and socially and environmentally sustainable". And as James Gustave Speth, the Administrator of UNDP said last year: "At UNDP, we are calling this new vision 'sustainable human development (SHD)'. We must wed sustainable development and human development and not just in words but in practice, every day, on the ground, around the world. Sustainable human development is development that doesn't merely generate growth, but distributes its benefits equitably; it regenerates the environment rather than destroying it; it empowers people rather than marginalizing them; it enlarges their choices and opportunities and provides for people's participation in decisions affecting their lives. Sustainable human development is development that is pro-poor, pro-nature, pro-jobs, and pro-women. It stresses growth, but growth with employment, growth with environment, growth with empowerment, growth with equity. Sustainable human development is not just a UNDP slogan; it is a unifying concept for all of us engaged in the business of development cooperation."

Sustainable human development is people-centered development that is socially just, ecologically sustainable, politically participatory, economically productive, and culturally vibrant. What is most significant about this is not that you and I agree with this statement, but that it is the global consensus of the international community.

Within this comprehensive framework, UNDP has decided to focus its efforts on five impact areas – poverty alleviation, productive employment and livelihoods, advancement of women and other disadvantaged groups, environmental regeneration, and participatory governance, which undergirds the other four. Within each country, strategic entry points are being identified by the government and the civil society. These can be, for example, HIV/AIDS, basic education, the urban environment, the role of the private sector, gender, public sector management, and so forth. From a given entry point, dialogue is stimulated among the relevant social actors concerning new policies, programs, and projects that link the five impact areas and move the society towards social equity and ecological balance. Harmonization of the social system and the natural system is what is needed.

But this vision is not just a UNDP vision. Because of the positive response of the other agencies of the UN system to this vision, the Secretary-General has asked the Administrator of UNDP to coordinate all UN development activities within an SHD framework.

Once the concept of SHD is somewhat clear, the question becomes, how can it be operationalized? But SHD is a holistic *vision*. Some of us at UNDP have argued that we cannot simply operationalize a vision, but that each country and community must first analyze its enhancing and inhibiting factors and create strategies and action plans for implementation in policies, program, and projects. This process requires activities both upstream at the level of policy and systems' design as well as downstream at the project, problem-solving level. I have suggested that this be called "facilitating a process of participation and partnership for sustainable human development".

One example of SHD is the LIFE Program, which I had the privilege of designing along with my colleague Shabbir Cheema, and for which I am the technical coordinator. With the entry point of urban environmental improvement, LIFE promotes "local-local" dialogue of the social actors – the NGOs, local government and community-based organizations (CBOs) (participatory governance), income generation (poverty alleviation and livelihoods) and the advancement of women, at the local/national, regional and inter-regional levels. At the local/country level, LIFE supports small-scale projects such as canal rehabilitation in Songkhla City, Thailand, sewerage improvement in Mitha Tiwana, Pakistan, garbage removal campaigns in Beni Suef, Egypt, and environmental education in a Rio de Janeiro slum. Each pilot country has a national coordinator, usually from a national NGO, and a national selection committee which is a partnership of local government, NGOs, CBOs, national government, the private sector, and international organizations. At the regional and inter-regional levels LIFE is supporting documentation, interchange and transfer by NGO networks and cities' associations of successful approaches of urban environmental improvement, including the transfer of the garbage pickers organizational model from Cairo to Bombay and Manila. At the global level, LIFE is a partnership of UNDP, the World Health Organization (WHO), the Governments of Sweden, the Netherlands, Germany, Denmark, the UK and the USA, and global NGO networks and cities' associations.

One critical dimension of SHD is the building of national and local capacities. Recently, at the request of my divisional director, I prepared a paper which suggested that the three skills most needed by national and local actors are systems thinking, strategic design and catalyzing multi-actor modalities of dialogue and action. Systems thinking allows holistic analysis, escaping narrow sectoral thinking. Strategic design moves beyond problem-solving to designing the future through strategic planning such as the Technology of Participation (ToP). And catalyzing multi-actor partnerships involves the identification of the stakeholders in any issue and facilitating their ongoing "multilogue" and collaboration to address specific issues or cross cutting ones. In addition, of course, other skills are needed by local and national

actors, including administrative and financial management
and infrastructural maintenance.

III.   The Role of NGOs in SHD
What then is the role of non-governmental organizations in
operationalizing SHD? To answer this, we must review the
complementary roles of each of the social actors. What is
the role of government, the private sector, community-
based organizations, and NGOs?

The role of government is to provide a society with legislation, with an executive, an administration, a bureaucracy,
and a judiciary. The role of government is to be concerned
about the well being of all the people, whether rich or poor,
whether powerful or weak. The role of government is to
set the rules of the game and to maintain orderly conduct
in relation to those rules. The role of government is to be
responsive and accountable to all the people.

The role of the private sector is to provide goods and
services, to promote economic activity, to provide trade and
commerce, to provide jobs, to produce and to distribute.

The role of community-based organizations (CBOs) is to
promote the interests of local people, to promote the perspective of local people, to care for local neighborhoods,
families, and individuals and to express the uniqueness of
local people.

The role of NGOs is to protect the interests of a particular group of people, to advocate policy options, to act as an
intermediary between other social actors, to provide training
and capacity building, to provide services which are not being

adequately provided by the other sectors, to implement pilot projects, and to test approaches of problem-solving or future design.

The challenge is to maintain the complementary interplay of these various social actors. This is an emerging definition of governance – the facilitation of a healthy interaction of the social actors towards sustainable human development. Each of the social actors has a role to play in governance and a responsibility to seek good governance and to move the society towards SHD.

There is a growing awareness within the international community of the vital importance of a vibrant civil society for a healthy nation or community. A civil society is made of a wide range of NGOs, CBOs, trade unions and interest groups. Countries with a high Human Development Index have a highly developed and active civil society. In the past few years, the UN has sought the active participation of NGOs and CBOs in UN conferences and in UN programs and projects. NGO presence was a powerful force at the Earth Summit in Rio in 1992 and the Population Summit in Cairo in 1994 and will be a powerful force in the Social Summit in Copenhagen and the Women's Summit in Beijing in 1995 and the City Summit in Istanbul in 1996. But, participation in global and national dialogue is only part of the role of NGOs.

As indicated earlier the world community is reaching a high degree of consensus on what constitutes sustainable human development and NGOs have been involved in creating that consensus. What is needed now is for NGOs to design their own strategies and action plans to implement

the global consensus at the national and local levels. The bat-
tle is no longer at the conceptual level but has shifted to the
placing of SHD into projects, programs, and policies. NGOs
are being called to act as facilitators of the process of participatory partnerships towards sustainable human development. UNDP has recently prepared a strategy paper on the
role of NGOs in development and is working to allow NGOs
not only to implement UN programs through sub-contracts
but to act as an executing agency or the primary contractual
party which heretofore has been reserved for UN agencies
and national governments. This will mean that NGOs will be
able to design and manage UN programs.

IV. Role of the ICAI in SHD
This leads me naturally to the role of the ICAI in facilitating
processes of participation and partnership towards sustainable human development. As you know well, the ICAI has a
great legacy of approaches for which the world is in need
and is actively searching. Every day in my work, I see that the
world needs contextual re-education, social re-formulation,
and spirit re-motivation. The world needs contexts which
are comprehensive, future-looking, archaic and intentional,
effective methods of discussion and planning, imaginal education, and depth reflection, an enabling style that affirms
the inherent possibility present in every organization, every
community and every person and a profound stance of gratitude for the mystery of life and compassion for all beings.
UNDP, for example, among many, many organizations, is
beginning to utilize the Technology of Participation (ToP).

A few examples of ICA staff and former staff that I have contracted as UNDP consultants are as follows. When I left New York last week, Eunice Shankland was designing a training course at UNDP on Sustainable Human Development which will be a pilot for use with all our 131 country offices, and had helped design and facilitate a briefing session for 18 new Resident Representatives, in a training course, along with Mirja Hansen, for our new Sustainable Development Advisers in 30 country offices, each of whom had a copy of *Winning Through Participation*. When I return, I will facilitate the module in this course on Governance. Jan Sanders last month helped facilitate the International Workshop for the LIFE National Coordinators. The LIFE National Coordinators are asking for more training in participatory methods. Kevin Balm and Raul Jorquera recently facilitated a regional workshop for the Global Environment Facility's Small Grant Program in Latin America and the Caribbean. Richard Alton and Bryan Fisher facilitated a similar program for the Global Environment Facility (GEF) in Africa. And, Kevin Balm also facilitated the GEF regional workshop for Asia and the Pacific.

In January of this year, Mary D'Souza helped facilitate the Global Advisory Committee Workshop in Stockholm for the LIFE Program. Before that Mary helped evaluate UNDP's global program promoting the role of women in water and sanitation projects. ICA Egypt designed and trained the facilitators for the LIFE National Consultation in Suez last year. Vaughn O'Halloran has also recently facilitated two workshops at UNDP Headquarters. UNDP has been in discussion with John Patterson about strategic management programs in Mongolia. And, Goran Hyden helped prepare a paper for UNDP entitled "A Practitioners Guide to Operationalizing Sustainable Human Development" in which the critical concept of "social capital" was put forward – the building up of relationships among people, i.e., partnerships. UNDP is becoming more aware everyday that it needs methods of facilitation if it is to help facilitate SHD with 131 program countries and among the host of UN agencies.

Conclusion
In conclusion, I would like to say that the New Paradigm has arrived. We do not need to wait any longer. The only challenge worth taking is the challenge of "how". How does each national ICA, each individual consultant, and colleague within his or her context and assignment help operationalize sustainable human development? Whether one is concerned with building partnerships for sustainable development, grassroots approaches in transforming education, transformation designs for 21ˢᵗ Century organizations, or recovering depth human culture, what is needed is increasingly clear to more and more people and groups around the world. How to do what is needed is far less clear. Here is where there is a need to step into the fray and offer one's best question, ones most comprehensive context, ones most intriguing gesture, ones most passionate social artistry. The world is beckoning. What is being called for is the courage to risk and give our all in this the greatest adventure of whole system transition.

Facilitation of national and international policy dialogue is needed as well as community-based projects. To do this requires forgiveness or acceptance of the seemingly rigid social and organizational structures, the inflated egos, including ones own, the unsettling despair, and the rampant cynicism of the now. We must facilitate nothing less than the re-invention of society. We have invented poverty and environmental degradation, and we can invent social equity, and ecological harmony. We are called to use our social artistry to facilitate whole system design of the future.

Eight years ago, Joep van Arendonk called the ICA the "People of the Question." Today I would like to expand on that by saying that the persons associated with ICA are the "People of the Context, the Method, the Style, and the Stance" – the people who will respond to the call to facilitate sustainable human development in every situation and in every opportunity. In every structure, there are the sensitive and responsive people. A vast movement of awakened and caring people is networking in a kaleidoscope of partnership around our blue planet.

This is the moment. We can do no other. How does that go again?

These are the times! We are the people!

B.

"Sustainable Human Development in the Urban Environment: a Global Perspective"

ICA Seattle

Seattle, Washington, USA
4 April 1995

*T*he next year, on my way to Asia, I was invited to speak to a
group of ICA colleagues in Seattle, Washington, USA. Before
I gave this talk, I had already spoken to a group of graduate
students at Antioch University in Seattle. With the ICA group, I
shared a model of sustainable human development and some of

UNDP's experience in urban development. Following the talk, there was a discussion about rural and urban development.

Introduction

The United Nations Development Programme (UNDP) is the central coordinating and funding body for all the UN family of agencies. We have 193 offices around the world in developing countries. Last week, I was in Colombia starting a program in Cartagena on the Caribbean coast. Next week, I will be in Bangladesh, starting a similar program in Dhaka, so I was able to stopover in Seattle, thanks to my friends from the Whole Systems Design (WSD) program at Antioch University.

I was fortunate to meet Harold Nelson, the director of the Whole System Design program, in San Francisco in December 1993 at an International Healthy Cities conference, where Harold and I were on a panel with Hazel Henderson, author of *The Politics of the Solar Age*. I was fascinated with what Harold had to say about Whole Systems Design. I was impressed with the curriculum and approach used at Antioch and the WSD program. I am interested to learn more from the program and want to support it in any small way I can. Today, we had a great day out at Camp Long, with the misty rain falling. There was a wonderful freshness. It was not like rain in New York. It was not oppressive. There is something light about this side of the continent.

I thought we would spend some time tonight thinking together and dialoguing about what is sustainable human development. What is sustainability, what is humanness, and what is development, particularly in the urban context.

I want to get us thinking about sustainable human development conceptually, then apply it to the urban context, particularly in developing countries, where I have spent most of my professional life.

A Model of Sustainable Human Development

There are several paradigm shifts going on at this moment. The UN is not so much the catalyst as it is the reflector, reflecting these shifts back to us. In Rio de Janeiro, at the Earth Summit, sustainability became a very hot issue, concern for ozone depletion, global warming, biodiversity, the killing off of massive numbers of species on this planet because of the kind of development that has gone on, particularly in this century.

The population conference in Cairo was very much about empowerment. The old image was how do we control women, so they have fewer babies, with a variety of contraceptive measures. It was a control metaphor. But in Cairo, this turned upside down, to how do we empower women to take control over their own lives in employment, education, health, and credit, and so on. It shifted from a control metaphor to an empowerment metaphor. This is a fundamental shift in perception of population issues. It is about empowering people to make responsible decisions about their lives.

Most recently, in Copenhagen, at the World Summit on Social Development which took place a few weeks ago, the focus was on equity. The agenda was on poverty alleviation and social integration, productive employment, and livelihood because what we have now is jobless growth. We have economic growth – increasing GNP and GDP – but we have fewer jobs. However, the focus in Copenhagen was on what is equity, how do you catalyze systems of equity, including access to credit, education, and jobs in an equitable manner.

Next year, we are holding the City Summit in Istanbul in June 1996 on human settlements and urban development – the Secretary General has named it the City Summit. We will be focusing directly on the future of cities. Are cities sustainable? How can we help make them sustainable? How can cities be more viable places for human habitation?

This little series of global conferences is not so much creating these changes in perception as reflecting them back to us. It is a feedback loop, and therefore it is reinforcing this shift in paradigm, world view, and perception of what is real, what is happening on our planet.

At UNDP, we have been talking for the last few years about sustainable human development. Heretofore, development has been very much in the production-consumption-economic paradigm. Development has been about increasing production by increasing consumption and the relationship between the two, and therefore is very much an economic driven model.

Our question is: How do we put people at the center of development – the well-being of people, all the people, the poor and children and women, and the ethnic groups. The question we ask governments these days is: How are your people doing? Not: What is your GNP? The World Bank previously had very much kept the focus on GNP and other macro economic indicators. We think the dialogue must shift to quality measures of social development and how is the life of people in a country, both the villages and the cities.

I like the way Willis Harman is talking about this shift, and others such as Joep van Arendonk in UNFPA. This is a critical shift from an economic paradigm to a human centered picture of development. The question is how you put that into policies, programs, and projects, a people centered approach.

The way Willis talks about it is to shift from putting "things" at the center – cars, jet airplanes, toothpaste, and other things – to putting people at the center. [diagram]. Let us put people at the center and around it, Planet Earth, because development must also be planet centered. You must have concern for our species along with other species and the life-support systems of our planet – soil, water, air, and so on. So, we have this complementarity of a people-centered and planet-centered development paradigm.

Around that we have the social actors: the public sector, the private sector, the voluntary sector, and the local sector. So you move from people and planet centered to ensuring the engagement and partnership of the social actors and then also the social sectors – the economic, the political, the cultural, and the environmental – to ensure comprehensiveness and inclusiveness.

At UNDP, we have suggested four foci to unite the UN system because it has many specialized agencies, such as ILO for labor, the World Bank with macro-economic indicators, WHO for health, UNICEF with women and children. UNDP is

a multisectoral, interdisciplinary organization, so we are trying to project a larger, integrative picture.

Here, we are saying we must focus on poverty alleviation
directly, environmental regeneration, gender sensitivity to
ensure the full partnership of over half the population on
this planet, which in many countries is not fully participating
at every level of society.

Have you seen the recent research that men and women
think differently? It is wonderful. We finally discovered this.
Did you know that? I did not. Now we can tell in the brain
where this light lights up here for men and there for women.
Jean Houston says that this may be *the* most significant revolution in the last 5,000 years, the full partnership of women
and men as the human perspective in civilization, so that it
affects every dimension and aspect of human society.

Then there is productive employment. People must face
this fact, that not all people have or can have employment,
but they can have a livelihood. How do you sustain yourself
and your family? We have so monetized our society that if we
do not have the stuff, we've out of a future. There was a time
when there was not money. It was not too long ago. Money
has become divorced from human value. What is production?

In the book on the values revolution, the author talks
about why is it that a man's silk necktie is something appro-
priate to produce? Is that a value? What is the value of this
thing hanging around your neck?

I was in a historic cities conference last year in Fez,
Morocco, speaking on the role of culture in urban development. One evening, I was sitting with some colleagues from

the World Bank. I said something outrageous. I think I had had too much wine. I said: Gold has no intrinsic value. How do we have a people-centered monetary system?

Last week in Colombia, I visited a man in a slum in Cartagena, living in a shack near a polluted swamp. Why is his life not more important than a room full of gold, more valuable, more precious? Who decides what is of value – a silk necktie, a jet plane, a human being, your life, my life? Who is setting the values? We have become so thing oriented.

Now, with the dollar collapsing, people are buying gold. We are going back to a gold economy. Who decided gold had any value? It is a shiny metal.

At the heart of this model is governance. UNDP believes that good governance, participatory governance, undergirds all of these. Governance that involves all the social actors, in a collaborative, not confrontational, mode is what is called for. Governance is required that alleviates poverty, that produces jobs and supports livelihood, that renews the environment, that is gender sensitive.

Around this picture, you have a circle of entry points. You can enter this system from any place. For example, you can enter from the private sector, from looking at labor, at urban development. But once you enter, you are suddenly thrown into this whole system of sustainable, human-centered development. The different UN organizations enter from different points – UNICEF from the entry point of children, ILO through labor, World Bank through macro-economic indicators and so on.

The approach I am promoting is bringing systems thinking, strategic design, process consulting, and multi-actor partnerships into the model. Systems thinking is very much what we are looking at in the Whole Systems Design Program. Strategic Design – the ICA's *Technology of Participation* is one of the finest approaches of this on the planet, although there are others.

You may say: Isn't this all rather abstract? Yes, it is. It is a model. My wife likes to talk about the way a hologram is produced. It looks as though something is there, but it is a photon. You can not touch it. I do not understand it entirely. Does anyone know?

Bill Norton: You use a laser. When you reflect it, you get two perspectives recorded at once.

Yes. The laser is pure light and the other is refracted light. Then there is a plate where the whole is in every part and suddenly this three-dimensional object appears before your eyes. You can walk around it and look at it. Have you all seen holograms? We are now into virtual reality.

The point is that a model is like the pure light of the laser that is a referent beam. Of course, it is abstract. You want your model to be comprehensive, future-oriented, intentional, and archaic. So, when you walk into a village or city or company or NGO, you have something in the back of your head. You have a perspective, and therefore you can bump into the real situation because you have a comprehensive, abstract model of the dynamics and their relationships.

Some of you were at the ICA International conference at Lonavala, India, last October, when we talked about this. That was immensely helpful in elaborating on this model. I developed this model because somebody asked me to make a presentation in another division, so I thought we ought to have a comprehensive model. Then the training department picked it up, and they made these slides and now people are using it all over the organization.

This means that even in a bureaucracy as large as the UN, you can enter the system anywhere. You can perturb the system through a sub-system and inject a creative idea or model or insight or method, and that can begin to move the system. I think this is an especially important insight about creativity and responsibility, wherever you are.

The Evolution of Urbanization
Our species is about two million years old and homo sapiens is about 50,000 years. We have been a rural species for about two million years until the 20th century. By the year 2,000, 51% of the human species will live in cities and towns. At the beginning of this century, 20% of us lived in cities and towns. So, this has happened in one century, after two million years, and you wonder why we are all so confused and disoriented. That is just one sort of revolution.

Let us talk about a few others.

Urbanization is an inevitable, irreversible trend of civilization, or so it appears to us at the United Nations. Many countries have tried through policies to stem the rural-urban migration, but they have all failed because there are too many push and pull factors driving people out of rural areas – famine, drought, desertification, poor living conditions, lack of infrastructure, lack of health care, and so on.

Then there are those forces attracting people to the cities. Not only the bright lights, but the better infrastructure of health care, employment opportunities, educational opportunities for women. So, this appears to be an inevitable and irreversible trend. Where this trend is taking place most rapidly is not in the "developed" world. This has been urban for some time, such as in the United States, Canada, and Europe. It is happening in the "developing" world. Urbanization is happening faster in Africa than anywhere else. The largest percentage of people living in cities and towns is in Latin America. The largest absolute number of people in urban areas is in Asia and the Middle East.

Urbanization has got a bad name. We say that cities bring crime and violence and disorientation and alienation and poverty and environmental degradation. All the above is true. Urbanization has many negative impacts. But urbanization has also brought with it many positive factors. People live longer in urban areas. Birth rates go up and death rates go down. Longevity goes up. There are more educational opportunities and better health care, more employment opportunities, more cultural opportunities.

So, urbanization has both plus and minus factors. The question then is: What is your strategy? How are you going to deal with both those factors? It appears there is a certain level of urbanization necessary for development. You see that in "developing" countries where over 60% of GNP is generated from cities and towns, even where it is an exceedingly small percentage in some of the "least developed countries" such as Tanzania. So, it becomes a challenge to "accentuate the positive and eliminate the negative" as in the old song. How do you respond to urbanization as a challenge, not as a problem, for what urbanization offers us?

UNDP's Strategies for Urban Development
At UNDP, we talk to national governments and listen to municipal officials, we suggest a strategy that involves urban poverty elimination; that you provide credit for people who do not have collateral such as the Grameen Bank in Bangladesh is doing; that you provide access to basic services of water, sanitation, health, education; that you promote various approaches to income generation and the concept of livelihood as a basket of activities – you might sell certain things on the sidewalk and other types of income generating activities because there might never be enough jobs per se, particularly at this time in the history of "developing" countries.

In addition to poverty alleviation, the second point in the UNDP strategy is the provision of infrastructure and services. This must be faced head on in the cities. What you have is incredible. Let us take Dar-es-Salaam, the Tanzanian capital. Dar-es-Salaam has one of the fastest rates of growth of any city in the world. When you go there, people think that the real city is the one that has sanitation services and paved streets and electrification. But that is only 30% percent of the population. There is a little island that people think is the real Dar-es-Salaam. But it is the surrounding area that is the real Dar-es-Salaam.

It is the same for the economy. 80% of the people in Dar-es-Salaam work in the informal economy but that is seen as

something extraneous. The formal economy, the government and private sector jobs account for only 20% of the
jobs. People are earning their livelihood on the streets, selling stuff and all kinds of activity. So, the real city is the city of
the informal sector and the informal settlements, the slums
and squatter zones. The formal city is the artificial city, the
city of the elite, of the government bureaucrats.

If we have a people-centered urban development strategy, how do we put the focus on the 70% of the people who
do not have a voice? How do we change the equation so
that that happens? In addition, you must strengthen local
government – local government capacities, the ability to
generate revenue, property taxes and other mechanisms of
revenue generation. Many cities are not allowed to be self-
sufficient. New York City is not allowed to be self-sufficient.
So much of its money goes to Albany and Washington DC
and across the country. NYC could be a self-sufficient city if
we could keep our revenue, but it goes to the state and the
nation.

In many "developing" countries, it is not just a question of
financial administration and revenue. It also involves administrative capacity and management capacity; a whole range
of management skills is needed because of the low salaries,
not only of municipal government but of central government. Civil servants often have little motivation. There must
be a whole reformulation of civil service.

The urban environment is the fourth focus in the UNDP
urban strategies. We must focus directly on solid waste management, liquid waste management, air pollution, water

pollution, occupation of hazard prone areas since many of the poor are living in dangerous areas.

In the slum I visited in Cartagena, raw sewage is flowing directly into the swamp and from there directly into the Caribbean. Children are playing in open sewers, so you can imagine the health hazards.

Finally, we are suggesting we must promote the full role of NGOs and the private sector in urban management. City government can not provide all the services. You need community-based organizations, non-governmental organizations, civil society organizations (CSOs), private entrepreneurs, private companies, and you need to divide things up so things will happen. In the USA, we assume there are volunteer groups for everything, and there often are. It is the power and strength of this society. It is critical to bring these in. It can be a little dangerous for the private sector.

In Cartagena, I was leaving the mayor's office, and there was a demonstration in front of his office. About 300 public workers were demonstrating because they were going to lose their jobs because the city government was hiring a Spanish company to collect waste. My colleague and I walked out, and they thought we were the Spanish entrepreneurs. They all started walking toward us, 300 people chanting and waving their banners. I thought: This is the end. I was expecting this crowd to descend on us and tear us apart. But we made it through. So be careful when you privatize, so people do not think you are the bad guy. But clearly, the private sector can and must play a role in the provision of services in urban development.

That is a just a brief sketch of the five thrusts of our urban development strategy. I want to end by sharing with you some of the work I am doing in an urban environmental improvement program called LIFE – Local Initiatives Facility for the Urban Environment. It is a small program with $12 million funds. We are working in 20 countries. What is exciting about it is that I was able to help design it using my 23 years of ICA experience and methods.

It is very much focused on participatory methods, and partnership methods, using many of the models from our history.

It is exciting to see that the august United Nations is listening to an NGO – I come from a humble NGO background.

Remember the impact of NGOs in the Rio conference. And now in Copenhagen, NGOs are an even more powerful presence, and increasingly so. The UN is very eager and knows it must, even as a club of nation states, have strong partnerships with NGOs, and the private sector. The private sector already may be determining the future of our planet. When the US government tries to control the collapse of the dollar against the yen and the Deutsche Mark. It throws in a billion dollars, two billion dollars and nothing really happens. A trillion dollars is being exchanged every day. So, the US government cannot control the value of the dollar. The Japanese government cannot control it. Hazel Henderson talks about the stock market as a global roller coaster of electronic money, funny money.

What is happening with the global economy is just out of control.

UNDP's LIFE Program

The LIFE program was launched at the Earth Summit in Rio. We selected two countries per region and now we are in three countries per region: in Latin America, we are in Brazil, Colombia, and Jamaica; in Africa, we are in Tanzania, South Africa, and Senegal; in the Middle East, in Morocco, Egypt, and shortly Lebanon; and in Asia, in Pakistan, Thailand, and Bangladesh. We are starting now in Eastern Europe, in Kyrgyzstan, Albania, and part of Russia.

The idea of the program is to get people to talk together. We call it local-local dialogue. I spend a lot of time getting people to talk with each other. We sit down and talk with local government, NGOs, community grassroots groups from the slums, and the private companies, getting these people to sit around the table, form task forces and to launch pilot projects. We are getting an enthusiastic response and the donors, mostly from Europe – Sweden, the Netherlands, Germany, and Denmark – are pleased. The United States has not bought into this yet, but we are hoping it will.

The UNDP, traditionally, has worked at the central government level. The UN Resident Representative is the highest-ranking diplomat in any country. He or she is the highest UN official representing all the UN agencies in any country. That person traditionally has worked at the level of the prime minister, president, cabinet, and ministries. Increasingly, what is happening is that the UN is waking up to the fact that you can not do development only from the top. You must also do it at the bottom and the middle and all the way down the line (if you use a vertical model, which is not correct). The pyramid is not the way it really works, is it? The pyramid is another paradigm.

So, in each of these countries there is a national LIFE task force with all these actors represented. There is a national coordinator recruited locally. This is different from many UN programs which have international experts sitting in the country or coming in and out. We recruit national coordinators from the national/local NGO community. The national task force identifies pilot projects, and then provide seed funding for a variety of projects from canal rehabilitation in Thailand, to solid waste management/garbage collection/recycling in Cairo, to a company working on coastal pollution in Colombia.

This is a small program to date. Twelve million dollars is little. But it is not a joke, if you believe that you can catalyze systemic change from anywhere within the system. Do you believe that? That is the question, is it not? How do you do that? Where do you place yourself, so that you provoke systemic change, whether at the micro level, the mesa level, or the macro level, in whatever sector? This is a question of strategy, of design, of one's style, how one interacts with different institutions.

Group Dialogue
I think I will stop here, because I want to hear what is going on in Seattle, with you, your concerns about sustainable, human development, particularly in the urban context, your dreams, your comments.

Q. How do you reconcile the top part of your chart which is talking about the incremental growth of urban centers and strategies that are making urban centers more attractive?

Nancy Lanphear: About ten years ago, we were working in an urban slum in Nairobi which started in 1976 with 20,000 people and ten years later had 40,000 people. But it worked because there was participation in education, in employment and community organization. The country was so pleased that they said to go ahead and work in the rural, so we had projects all over the place. It made a difference in the country. It was very visible, and people could come and see it. It was part of a national strategy. It worked because it helped to organize massive of numbers of people coming into the urban in a small area.

Rob Work: It is a valid question. That is why you also must have a rural development strategy. I did not talk about that. Of course, there is a rural-urban continuum. You can not separate them. It is one system or habitat spectrum. What is rural and what is urban differs from country to country. If you believe that urbanization is inevitable and irreversible, you must deal with the quality of life in urban areas while at the same time you develop rural areas.

Development has a bias towards the rural. If you look at the last thirty years of development, most projects, as with the ICA, were in the rural areas. We saw very clearly that there was tremendous innocent suffering in rural areas. There was and there still is.

We also had some projects in urban areas. The question is one of strategy. My point is the bias is toward the rural. In development circles, most projects have been in rural areas because people felt that cities were already developed. They had better infrastructure and services. Cities are growing, one way or the other, but poverty is also increasing. In Latin America, 90% of the poor live in cities. That may surprise you because there is also a lot of poverty in the rural areas.

Again, it is the poor who are being driven out of rural areas and traveling to the urban. They end up living on the periphery of cities in shanty towns without services but working extremely hard. I have lived in some slums. People put every penny they had into improving their house. They are out there working every day. They are not sitting around doing nothing.

Q. What does development of rural areas look like?
Rob Work: What we are also telling people is that one way to relieve the pressure on the megacities is by stimulating the growth of medium sized cities, so they can act as population growth poles in rural areas, so that everybody doesn't go to the national capital. You can then have more regionalized population centers.

Jim Jewell: A lot of so-called rural development is agro-business which has simply driven more people out of rural areas. Large corporations are doing this. I was also reflecting on what you mean by urban. Thirty-five million people in Mexico City and 20,000 in some other places.

Work: Yes, that is a rather large range, is it not? We are calling cities with over ten million people megacities. The number of megacities is growing. We are facing a scale of problems we have never faced before in human history, to provide so many jobs and avenues of livelihood, so much water, and so on. It is an incredible leap in human inventiveness that is required. We have never had to care for that many human beings in such a concentrated geographic area.

What surprises me the most about cities is that they work as well as they do. When I think about it, I imagine total breakdown. That they function at all, always amazes me. There is something about self-organizing systems. By and large, human settlements are self-organizing. Even in policy, growth policies and development policies at various levels with various stimulants and mechanisms to try and move people often do not work well. People really vote with their feet. They just get out and go.

Bill Norton: Back to the question of what is rural development? My experience of doing rural development is that the kinds of things you usually have to deal with are health care systems, so that people don't have to leave their villages to have access to a good clinic or a local health caretaker. This was true in the kind of project I was involved with in the Ivory Coast in West Africa. Often small industries are key. The Trickle Up program provided small cash incentives to people to start a project: to not just be a primary producer but do some of the manufacturing; to grow sisal but also weave the mat, make baskets; some very micro scale industries, plus health care and education. If you do those kinds of things, among others, the people in a village are usually very quick to figure out what they can do. A lot of it has to do with schooling and infrastructure, roads, access to get to the cities to shop and come back, in an affordable manner.

Linda VerNooy: I want to give another example of rural development in a village in Peru, outside Lima. When people asked the village what they wanted in terms of development, the first thing they were really interested in was building up their identity. They wanted a little plaza in their village with a television so they could watch TV together instead of trying to buy one for each of their homes. Once they worked on that kind of project, the participation of the community in other projects increased about 80%. Once they built up their identity, they then moved into infrastructure and water systems and irrigation.

Sharon Fisher: Another aspect of that that comes to mind was when I worked in a rural village in the Philippines. It was extremely critical that we worked in bringing the community together.

Bibliography
For Further Reading

Publications

Berry, Thomas, and Brian Swimme.1994. *The Universe Story*. San Francisco: Harper One.

Bregman, Rutger. 2020. *Humankind: A Hopeful History*. New York: Little, Brown and Co.

_____. 2016. *Utopia for Realists*. Amsterdam: The Correspondent.

Canfield, Jack, Mark Victor Hansen, and Jennifer Read Hawthorne. 2007. *Life Lessons for Loving the Way You Live*. Deerfield Beach: Health Communications.

Cheema, G. Shabbir, ed. 2003. *Reinventing Government for the Twenty-First Century*. Boulder: Kumarian.

Cheema, G. Shabbir, and Vesselin Popovski, eds.2010. *Engaging Civil Society*. Tokyo: UN University Press.

Cooperrider, David L. 2005. *Appreciative Inquiry*. San Francisco: Berrett-Koehler.

Dalai Lama, 14th.2001. *Ethics for the New Millennium.* New York: Riverhead Books.

Eisenstein, Charles. 2011. *Sacred Economics.* Berkeley: Evolver Editions.

Emmott, Stephen. 2013. *Ten Billion.* New York: Vintage.

Gandhi, Mohandas. 1993. *Gandhi: An Autobiography—The Story of My Experiment with Truth.* New York: Beacon.

Goleman, Daniel. 2005. *Emotional Intelligence.* New York: Bantam.

Hansen, James. 2009. *Storms of My Grandchildren.* New York: Bloomsbury

Harman, Willis. 1990. *Global Mind Change.* New York: Grand Central.

Hock, Dee. 2000. *Birth of the Chaordic Age.* Oakland: Berrett-Koehler.

Houston, Jean. 2004. *Jump Time.* Boulder: Sentient Publications

_____. 1982. *The Possible Human.* Los Angeles: J. P. Tarcher.

King, Martin Luther, Jr. 2010. *Strength to Love.* Minneapolis: Fortress.

Klein, Naomi. 2017. *No Is Not Enough.* Chicago: Haymarket Books.

_____2014. *This Changes Everything: Capitalism vs. the Climate.* New York: Simon & Schuster Paperbacks.

Kolbert, Elizabeth. 2014. *The Sixth Extinction: An Unnatural History.* New York: Henry Holt.

Korten, David C. 1995. *When Corporations Rule the World.* Boulder: Kumarian and Berrett-Koehler.

Lawrence, D. H. 1959. *Selected Poems*. New York: Viking Compass.

Mandela, Nelson. 1995. *Long Walk to Freedom*. New York: Back Bay Books.

McKibben, Bill. 2011. *Eaarth: Making a Life on a Tough New Planet*. New York: St. Martin's Griffin.

Nelson, Harold. 2014. *The Design Way*. Boston: MIT Press.

Nhat Hanh, Thich. 1998. *The Heart of the Buddha's Teachings*. Berkeley: Parallax.

Owen, Harrison. 2008. *Open Space Technology*. San Francisco: Berrett-Koehler.

Ray, Paul H. 2000. *The Cultural Creatives*. New York: Three Rivers Press.

Reich, Robert B. 2016. *Saving Capitalism*. New York: Vintage.

Rifkin, Jeremy. 2009. *The Empathic Civilization*. New York: J. P. Tarcher/Penguin.

Rilke, Rainer Maria. 1986. *Letters to a Young Poet*. New York: Vintage.

Sanders, Bernie. 2016. *Our Revolution*. New York: Thomas Dunne Books.

Shantideva. 2003. *The Way of the Bodhisattva*. Boston: Shambhala

Stanfield, R. Brian. 2000. *The Art of Focused Conversation*. Toronto: The Canadian Institute of Cultural Affairs.

_____. 2012. *The Courage to Care*. 2nd Edition. Toronto: The Canadian Institute of Cultural Affairs.

_____. 2002. *The Workshop Book*. Toronto: The Canadian Institute of Cultural Affairs.

Staples, Bill. 2012. *Transformational Strategy*. Toronto: Canadian Institute of Cultural Affairs.

Teilhard de Chardin, Pierre. 1959. *The Phenomenon of Man*. New York: Harper Colophon Books.

Thunberg, Greta. 2019. *No One Is Too Small To Make A Difference*. New York: Penguin Books.

Timsina, Tatwa. 2012. *Changing Lives, Changing Societies*. Kathmandu: ICA Nepal.

United Nations Development Programme. 2012. *Human Development Report 2011*. New York: Palgrave Macmillan/ United Nations.

Ward, Larry. 2020. *America's Racial Karma: An Invitation to Heal*. Westminster MD: Parallax.

Warren, Elizabeth. 2014. *A Fighting Chance*. Metropolitan Books, New York.

Wilber, Ken. 2001. *A Brief History of Everything*. Boulder: Shambhala.

_____. 2007. *The Integral Vision*. Boulder: Shambhala.

Williams, R. Bruce. 2006. *More Than 50 Ways to Build Team Consensus*. Thousand Oaks: Corwin.

Work, Robertson. 2007. "Strengthening Governance and Public Administration Capacities for Development: A UN Background Paper." New York: United Nations.

Yousafzai, Malala. 2015. *I Am Malala*. New York: Back Bay Books.

Websites
350.org
ACLU, www.aclu.org

A Compassionate Civilization (blog,) http://compassiona-
    tecivilization.blogspot.com/
Big History Project, www.bighistoryproject.com/home
Building Creative Communities Conference https://www.
    bc3-colquittga.com
Charter for Compassion, www.charterforcompassion.org
Democracy Now, www.democracynow.org/
Democracy Spring, www.democracyspring.org
Disruption, watchdisruption.com
Emberling, Dennis. 2005. "Stages of [Leadership] Development."
www.developmentalconsulting.com/pdfs/Stages_of_
    Development_vA.pdf
Greenpeace, www.greenpeace.org/international/en
Gross National Happiness, http://www.gnhcentrebhutan.
    org/what-is-gnh/
Horace Mann School (NYC) https://www.horacemann.org/
Human Rights Watch, www.hrw.org
ICA Social Research Center/Archives: www.icaglobalar-
    chives.org
IndivisibleGuide.com, www.indivisibleguide.com
Institute of Cultural Affairs (ICA) International, www.ica-
    international.org
Institute of Cultural Affairs USA www.ica-usa.org
Integral Institute, in.integralinstitute.org/integral.aspx
International Association of Facilitators (IAF), www.iaf-
    world.org/site
Kosmos, www.kosmosjournal.org
New York University (NYU) Wagner Graduate School of
    Public Service, wagner.nyu.edu

Oklahoma City University https://www.okcu.edu

One World House, oneworldhouse.net

Our Revolution, ourrevolution.com

Pale Blue Dot, www.youtube.com/watch?v=p86BPM1GV8M

Peoples Climate, peoplesclimate.org

People's Summit, www.thepeoplessummit.org

Social Artistry, www.jeanhouston.org/Social-Artistry/social-
    artistry.html

Story Bridge https://www.storybridge.space/

Swamp Gravy https://swampgravy.com/

Technology of Participation (ToP) Network, icausa.member-
    clicks.net

"The Story of Solutions", www.youtube.com/watch?v=
    cpkRvc-sOKk

Transition Towns, www.transitionus.org/transition-towns

UN Department of Economic and Social Affairs (UNDESA),
    www.un.org/development/desa/en

UNDESA Public Service Awards and Global Forum https://
    publicadministration.un.org/en/UNPSA

UN-Habitat, unhabitat.org

UN Intergovernmental Panel on Climate Change www.ipcc.
    ch

United Nations Development Programme, www.undp.org

United Nations Millennium Development Goals https://
    www.un.org/millenniumgoals/

United Nations Sustainable Development Goals,

www.un.org/sustainabledevelopment/sustainable-
    development-goals

Universal Declaration of Human Rights, www.un.org/en/
    universal-declaration-human-rights/
World Fair Field International Festival https://worldfairfield.
    org/

About the Author

Speaking at ICA USA in Chicago in 2010: Photo by Jim Troxel

Moorman Robertson Work, Jr. has worked in international develop-ment for over fifty years in over fifty countries. Recently, for ten years, he was a UN consultant, confer-ence speaker, New York University Wagner Graduate School of Public Service adjunct professor of inno-vative leadership, Fulbright Senior Specialist assisting universities overseas, and Fellow of the NYU Wagner Research Center for Leadership in Action. He is now a nonfiction author, and ecosystems/justice activist. This is his fourth book with contributions made to eleven others.

Previously, he was United Nations Development Programme (UNDP) deputy director of democratic gover-nance, and principal policy adviser of decentralized gover-nance for sixteen years at UN headquarters in New York. While with UNDP, he designed and coordinated the Local Initiative Facility for Urban Environment (LIFE) operating in twenty countries and another global program, Decentralizing the Millennium Development Goals (MDGs) through Innovative Leadership. He also coordinated a global community of practice on decentralized governance, provided policy advice to countries worldwide, conducted research and prepared global policy papers.

Prior to UNDP, Robertson served in Malaysia, Republic of Korea, Jamaica, Texas/Oklahoma, and Venezuela for twenty-one years as country and regional director with the Institute of Cultural Affairs (ICA), an international NGO with UN Economic and Social Council Consultative status. His work of human development has consisted of the design and implementation of research, training and demonstration projects in leadership, organizational, and community development, rural and urban development, NGO and project management, policy formulation and advice and group facilitation.

Work has written widely on decentralization and local governance, urban and rural development, poverty eradication and environmental improvement, the role of civil society in governance and development, capacity development and participatory methods. In addition to NYU, he has taught at the University of the West Indies, University of Aruba, Antioch University Graduate School of Whole System Design, the ICA Global Academy, and the Social Artistry School. He conducted his graduate studies at Indiana University and Chicago Theological Seminary and undergraduate studies at Oklahoma State University, which honored him in 2003 with its Distinguished Alumnus Award. He and his wife live in Swannanoa, North Carolina, near family, friends, the Blue

Ridge Mountains, and the Great Smoky Mountains. He continues to believe that an ecological-compassionate community, nation, and world are necessary and possible to create.

He may be contacted at robertsonwork100@gmail.
com. His blogsite is at: https://compassionatecivilization.
blogspot.com/

Made in the USA
Columbia, SC
10 December 2020